THE INDEPENDENT ~~~

UNIVERSAL ORLAN

G. COSTA

Limit of Liability and Disclaimer of Warranty:
The publisher has used its best efforts in preparing this book, and the information provided herein is provided "as is." Independent Guides and the author make no representation or warranties with respect to the accuracy or completeness of the contents of this book and specifically disclaim any implied warranties of merchantability or fitness for any particular purpose and shall in no event be liable for any loss of profit or any other commercial damage, including but not limited to special, incidental, consequential, or other damages.
Please read all signs and safety information before entering attractions, as well as the terms and conditions of any third party companies used. Prices are approximate, and do fluctuate.

Contents

In 1971, Orlando was put on the map as the theme park capital of the world with the opening of the Walt Disney World Resort. It was a place that families could visit together to make memories.

The Walt Disney World Resort was a giant version of the Disneyland Resort that had opened in 1955 in Anaheim, California.

In the late 1980s, Universal announced it too would get in on the thrill game too by opening its own East Coast theme park, similar to the one it had opened in Hollywood, California.

Disney saw this new theme park as a big competitor and decided that it would also build a theme park based around movie studios.

Miraculously, *Disney's MGM Studios* managed to open its doors in 1989, before the grand opening of Universal Studios Florida one year later. MGM was a rushed project; and *Universal Studios Florida* blew Disney's theme park away when it finally opened in 1990.

In 1995, the expansion of Universal Orlando began as the company invested billions of dollars to create a second theme park, *Universal's Islands of Adventure*. Three on-site resort hotels and an entertainment and dining district, *CityWalk*, were also constructed.

The original *Universal Studios Florida* park was also expanded with new areas to create a multi-day destination rivalling Disney.

In 1999, *Universal's Islands of Adventure* opened to rave reviews. It featured innovative attractions such as *The Amazing Adventures of Spider-Man* and *The Incredible Hulk Coaster* which win awards year after year, even to this day.

The Universal Orlando Resort has fast become *the* place to visit in Orlando. Innovative attractions and areas such as T*he Simpsons Ride* and *The Wizarding World of Harry Potter*, have sent visitor figures sky-rocketing. Collectively, both theme parks now welcome 16 million guests yearly.

2018 marks an exciting year for the resort with a new attraction opening - *Fast & Furious: Supercharged*, as well as the new on-site Aventura Hotel.

Getting the best Universal Orlando ticket is crucial, and the right choice can save you a lot of money. There are many different ticket options that can be purchased. In this section we dissect them all.

Guests from any country can buy advanced tickets. The easiest place to purchase these is the official Universal Orlando website at www.universalorlando.com. Guests who do not buy their tickets in advance can do so at the theme parks but prices are more expensive.

Ticket Types:
There are two types of tickets: a Single Park ticket allows you access to one park per day (either *Universal Studios Florida* or *Islands of Adventure* or *Volcano Bay* on any one day), and Park-to-Park tickets allow you to enter all the parks on the same day.

Multi-day Single Park tickets allow you to visit the parks on separate days, but you cannot visit more than one park on the same day (for that you need a Park-to-Park ticket).

One day tickets vary in price depending on the visit date - see universalticketcalendar. com - peak season tickets are more expensive than off-peak tickets. Multi-day tickets are priced the same regardless of when you visit.

Single Park tickets allow you to ride every attraction in a single park except the *Hogwarts Express*, which needs a Park-to-Park ticket.

You can upgrade any Single Park ticket to a Park-to-Park ticket for an additional $50. You need to decide whether the flexibility of moving between parks on the same day, and access to the *Hogwarts Express* are worth the extra cost.

Child prices apply to children aged 3 to 9 years old. Children under 3 get free admission into the theme parks (proof of age may be requested on entry). Prices exclude tax.

Multi-park tickets bought via Universal's website include a book with $150 of coupons. A Universal "convenience fee" of $2.15 is added to online bookings.

Getting your tickets:
Advanced Tickets can be picked up from 'Will Call'

kiosks at the theme parks, or printed at home. Tickets can also be mailed to you for an extra cost. You can also purchase tickets on the Universal Orlando app.

Save with advanced tickets:
All multi-day tickets are $20 cheaper when pre-purchased in advance online than at the theme parks.

The 'Will Call' machines at the front of the park can only be used to pick up advanced tickets. If you have not purchased in advance, you will need to wait in the ticket queue line to see a Team Member and buy your tickets, or book on the app or by phone.

You can buy tickets at any on-site hotel and save $20 on tickets compared to park prices.

Can I add extra days to my ticket later?
Yes. To add extra days to your park ticket visit Guest Relations at either park before your last day of admission expires. Here, your tickets can be upgraded for the difference in price. Adding an extra day can be very affordable.

Are there any more ways to get discounted tickets?
Your work HR department may be part of the Universal Fan Club. Membership is free and you get slightly discounted tickets.

In addition, there are other websites and ticket brokers that offer tickets at reduced prices. We recommend thoroughly checking the reputation of the website you are purchasing from if it is not the official Universal website. Avoid second-hand sales. One large, trusted ticket broker is UndercoverTourist.com.

Do international visitors get a discount?
European residents usually visit Orlando for longer than Americans. Therefore, Universal offers special, longer Universal Bonus and Explorer Tickets. These are

also sold online outside Europe in some locations, but are harder to find.

The 2018 price for a 2-Park Explorer Ticket is £257 per adult and £248 per child. A 3-park ticket (with access to *Volcano Bay Water Park*) is the same price as the 2-Park ticket. These tickets are also sold at brokers such as www.attraction-tickets-direct.co.uk and www.attractiontix.co.uk.

Can I buy a ticket only for Volcano Bay Water Park?
Yes. A *Volcano Bay Water Park* ticket on its own is $67.

Florida Resident Tickets

Florida Residents can take advantage of discounts on multi-day tickets. Proof of residency must be shown when picking up tickets and/or when entering the parks.

Florida residents visiting for more than 3 days in a year should strongly consider looking at annual passes.

A valid Florida ID must be shown for each ticket purchased when picking them up. Accepted IDs are:
• Florida driver's license
• Florida state-issued ID card (must have Florida address)
• Florida voter's registration card with corresponding photo ID
• College ID from a Florida college or university with corresponding photo ID

Florida Resident discounted tickets must be purchased online in advance and

collected at any ticket window at both theme parks; these tickets cannot be purchased at the gates.

At the time of writing, residents can get up to $50 off multi-day tickets. Florida Resident tickets are valid for up to 60 days.

Blackout dates apply to Florida resident tickets. These are:
• December 21st 2017 to January 3rd 2018
• March 23rd to April 7th 2018
• July 1st to July 31st 2018
• December 22nd to December 31st 2018

Florida Resident Annual Passes
Florida residents can get discounts on annual passes. 2-Park Pricing is as follows: Seasonal pass - $260, Power Pass - $320 plus tax; Preferred Pass - $350 plus

tax; and Premier Pass - $485 plus tax. 3-Park Pricing is an additional $99-$154.

These passes are exactly the same as the non-Florida resident annual passes, except Florida residents pay less for their passes.

Proof of residency must be shown when picking up the Florida resident annual pass and/or when entering the parks. A valid Florida ID must be shown for each annual pass purchased.

All 1 Day tickets are subject to seasonal pricing depending on the season of the visit - one day tickets are priced the same for both advanced tickets and those bought at the theme park ticket booths (gate prices). All multi-day tickets include a $20 discount for booking in advance versus the gate prices. Add $20 to these prices if you are planning on purchasing at the park gates.

---

1 Day:
Single Park (USF or IOA): Adult - $110 to $124 and Child - $105 to $119
Park to Park (USF & IOA): Adult - $165 to $179 and Child - $160 to $174

---

2 Days:
One Park Per Day (USF or IOA):
Adult - $199.99
Child - $189.99

Park to Park (USF & IOA):
Adult - $254.99
Child - $244.99

Park to Park (USF & IOA & VB):
Adult - $294.99
Child - $284.99

USF - Universal Studios Florida, **IOA** - Islands of Adventure, **VB** - Volcano Bay

---

3 Days:
One Park Per Day (USF or IOA):
Adult - $219.99
Child - $209.99

One Park Per Day (USF or IOA or VB):
Adult - $259.99
Child - $249.99

Park to Park (USF & IOA):
Adult - $274.99
Child - $264.99

Park to Park (USF & IOA & VB):
Adult - $314.99
Child - $304.99

---

4 Days:
One Park Per Day (USF or IOA):
Adult - $229.99
Child - $219.99

One Park Per Day (USF or IOA or VB):
Adult - $269.99
Child - $259.99

Park to Park (USF & IOA):
Adult - $284.99
Child - $274.99

Park to Park (USF & IOA & VB):
Adult - $324.99
Child - $314.99

---

5 Days:
One Park Per Day (USF or IOA):
Adult - $239.99
Child - $229.99

One Park Per Day (USF or IOA or VB):
Adult - $279.99
Child - $269.99

Park to Park (USF & IOA):
Adult - $294.99
Child - $284.99

Park to Park (USF & IOA & VB):
Adult - $334.99
Child - $324.99

Annual passes allow you to visit the resort as often as you wish (subject to blackout dates on some passes) at a very low per-visit price. In addition, special perks are offered to Passholders, including discounts on dining and merchandise.

	Seasonal Pass	Power Pass	Preferred Pass	Premier Pass
Pricing (for guests of all ages - excludes tax)	$284.99	$344.99	$384.99	$539.99
One Year of Unlimited Park-to-Park Admission	Blockout dates apply.	Blockout dates apply.	Yes	Yes
Early Park Admission	No	No	Blockout dates apply.	Yes
Free self-parking (after first visit)	No	50% off	Yes	Yes
Free valet and preferred self-parking (after first visit)	No	No	No	Yes
Discounts on theme park and special event tickets	Yes	Yes	Yes	Yes
One free Halloween Horror Nights ticket (Sun to Thurs)	No	No	No	Yes
Free admission to select special events (e.g. Mardi Gras)	No	Yes	Yes	Yes
Discounted food & merchandise	No	No	Yes	Yes
Discount on Blue Man tickets	Yes	Yes	Yes	Yes
Free CityWalk club access	No	No	No	Yes
Discounts at on-site hotels	Yes	Yes	Yes	Yes
Free Universal Express Pass (after 4:00pm)	No	No	No	Yes

Blockout dates for the Power Pass and Seasonal Pass:
These passes have dates that are blocked out (i.e. you can't enter the two theme parks).

• December 21st 2017 to January 3rd 2018

• March 23rd to April 7th 2018
• July 1st to 31st 2018
• December 22nd to 31st 2018.

Please note that Volcano Bay is also blocked out from July 1st to 31st 2018

All dates are inclusive.

On days that a concert is playing at *Universal Studios Florida* during a non-blockout date, then access will only be permitted to *Universal's Islands of Adventure.*

Getting There

Before the fun at Universal Orlando, you must first make your way there.

By Car

Address: *6000 Universal Blvd, Orlando, FL*. Universal Orlando is accessible by car from the Interstate 4 (I-4), where you follow *Universal Blvd* north to the parking area.

Parking garages open 90 minutes before the parks open. All levels except the top level are covered.

Self-parking is $20 per day, $25 for preferred and $35 for valet, 5-minute valet is $45. Disabled parking bays can be requested. These are closer to *CityWalk* and the theme parks. A drop-off point is also available.

Lunchtime visitors to *CityWalk* can get free valet parking by validating their restaurant receipt from Monday to Friday for two hours of free parking.

From 6:00pm to 10:00pm parking is $5. After 10:00pm, parking is free for all, except on peak dates such as *Halloween Horror Nights*.

After parking, go through security and walk through *CityWalk* – turn left for *Islands of Adventure* or right for *Universal Studios Florida*. Parking is 10 minutes' walk from the parks.

Disney to Universal Orlando by car:
Follow Disney resort signs to the Interstate 4 (I-4). Follow the *I-4 North/East* for 6 to 8 miles, take *exit 75A* and merge onto *Universal Blvd*.

Shuttle and Taxi Services

Mears and Super Shuttle are reliable shuttles, though other services are available. Prices are $30 to $35 per person roundtrip, or about $20 one-way.

A taxi with Mears Transportation is likely to cost $55-$70 with a tip each way per car. UberX is priced at about $28 to $34 from the airport to Universal.

Disney to Universal:
Super Shuttle quotes $45 for a 4-seater for a one-way trip, plus tip. A taxi is about $35, plus tip. UberX is $20 to $35.

Public Transportation

There are two options: *I-Ride Trolley* and *Lynx*. *I-Ride* follows a tourist route along *International Drive*; *Lynx* is a public bus system.

Both are about $2 per ride and the stop you want is called "International Drive and Visitors Circle". From there, it is a 20-minute walk to Universal.

From the bus stop, cross the road and head north on *Universal Blvd* until you reach the overhead walkway. Use this to enter Universal Orlando.

Disney to Universal:
Go to the *Transportation and Ticket Center (TTC)* or *Disney Springs*. Find the LYNX bus stop and catch the number 50 bus - get a transfer ticket.

Ride the bus for about 35 minutes the stop at *6800 Sea Harbor Dr and Central Florida Pky*.

Here, wait for the number 8 LYNX bus and ride it until *6200 International Dr and Universal Blvd*. The number 8 bus takes about 15 minutes (30 minutes at rush hour). From here, it is a 20-minute walk to the Universal Orlando Resort.

The journey time is about 1h15m to 1h30m.

Use Google Maps to plan this route - buses are not very regular.

Hotels

Deciding where you stay while on vacation can be tricky: you have to consider price, availability, size, location and amenities in order to find the perfect accommodation. Luckily, central Florida is renowned for having an incredible range of options to suit all tastes and budgets.

There are numerous hotels not located on Universal property that are more reasonably priced than the on-site options. However, for the full Universal Orlando experience, we recommend staying at one of the on-site hotels. You will be just minutes away from the action, and the benefits of staying on-site more than make up for the extra cost.

There are **three tiers** of on-site hotels:
• Prime Value – *Cabana Bay Beach Resort* and *Aventura Hotel*
• Preferred – *Royal Pacific Resort* and *Sapphire Falls Resort*
• Premier – *Portofino Bay Hotel* and *Hard Rock Hotel*

Benefits available to on-site hotel guests:
• Early entry to *The Wizarding World of Harry Potter* one hour before the park opens to regular guests and to *Volcano Bay*.
• Complimentary water taxis, shuttle buses and walking paths to both theme parks and Universal *CityWalk*.
• Complimentary delivery of merchandise purchased throughout the resort to your hotel.
• Resort-wide charging privileges. Swipe your credit card at check-in to use your room key to charge purchases to your room. At check-out, you will settle the balance as one amount.
• Complimentary Super Star Shuttle scheduled transportation to *SeaWorld* and *Aquatica*. This runs once a day from your hotel, and once or twice a day back to your hotel. Seats are reserved at concierge.
• Optional wake-up call from a Universal character.
• Use of the Golf Universal Orlando program.

Guests at *Royal Pacific Resort, Portofino Bay Hotel,* and *Hard Rock Hotel* also enjoy these added benefits:
• FREE Universal Express Pass - Unlimited ride access to skip the regular lines in both theme parks all day.
• Priority seating at select restaurants throughout both theme parks and *CityWalk*.

On-Site Amenities

In this section we cover all the essentials of staying at any of the five on-site Universal Orlando hotels. From parking to pet rooms, and transportation to toning up.

Parking:
Preferred and Premier hotels' parking is charged at $20 per night for self-parking and $27 per night for valet parking (plus tips). Hotel guests do not get a discount on this rate.

Day guests who park in the hotel lots pay $22 per day, unless eating in one of the on-site restaurants where they can have their parking validated for up to 3 hours of complimentary parking.

Parking charges at *Cabana Bay Beach Resort* and *Aventura Hotel* are $12 per night for hotel guests. Day guest parking prices vary.

Internet Access:
Standard in-room Wi-Fi access is complimentary. For higher speed access, there is a premium option at $15 per day.

The lobby and pool areas at all the on-site hotels have free Wi-Fi, which you can access regardless of whether you are staying at the hotel or not.

Pet rooms:
Pet rooms are available at all Premier and Preferred hotels, A cleaning fee of $50 per night applies, up to a maximum of $150 per room.

Refrigerators:
All rooms at all the on-site hotels include a complimentary mini-refrigerator.

Rooms at *Aventura Hotel* will also include a mini-fridge once the hotel opens.

Character Dining:
The *Royal Pacific Resort, Portofino Bay Hotel,* and *Hard Rock Hotel* offer character-dining experiences where characters visit your table for you to meet, chat and take photos, while you dine. At *Portofino Bay Hotel,* this is *Trattoria del Porto,* at *Hard Rock Hotel* this is *The Kitchen,* and at the *Royal Pacific Resort* you will find this at *Islands Dining Room.*

Characters vary from Scooby Doo to Shrek and even The Minions. Character dining takes place once or twice a week between 6:30pm and 9:30pm. You can visit any resort's restaurant, even if you are not a hotel guest.

Kids Activities:
Kids activities are available at *Royal Pacific Resort, Portofino Bay Hotel,* and *Hard Rock Hotel* in the evenings. This keeps kids occupied while parents spend quality time together.

Guests from any hotel can use the Kids Activities at other hotels. Details can be obtained from the concierge desk.

Prices are about $15 an hour.

FITNESS AND POOLS

Fitness Suites:
All five on-site hotels have complimentary fitness suites for their guests.

Although not widely advertised, guests staying at any on-site hotel can use any of the fitness suites.

This means that a guest from *Cabana Bay Beach Resort* could, for example, visit the gym at the *Hard Rock Hotel* with their room key.

Pools:
All the on-site hotels have impressive pools and you can 'pool hop'. Like the fitness suites mentioned above, if you are staying at any on-site resort hotel, you can use the pool of any resort. A fantastic benefit!

Who wouldn't want to try the fun pools at *Cabana Bay,* the magnificent one at the *Hard Rock,* and then finish the day with a dip at the new *Sapphire Falls* pool?

Aventura Hotel

This 600-room Prime Value hotel is priced for budget conscious guests. There are walking paths to the parks and CityWalk (20 to 25 minutes) or you can use the complimentary shuttle.

Room size: Standard rooms are 314 ft^2 and kids suites are 591 ft^2.

Room prices: From $164, plus tax for a standard room. Family suites are priced from $309, plus tax. Discounts apply for longer stays.

Activities: Arcade room; fitness center; pool and splash zone; a store; rooftop and poolside bars.

Set to open on August 16, 2018, *Aventura Hotel* will be the newest on-site property.

In contrast to all the other resorts which have elaborate themes, this hotel promises to be the most technologically advanced place to stay.

Rooms include all the amenities you would expect and some will even have views over and into the theme parks.

There will be a variety of food options - the food hall will feature a multitude of different cuisines. There will be no Table Service restaurant at this resort, however.

There are also three bars including one in the lobby, another on the roof offering amazing views, as well as a Starbucks.

Please note that complimentary Express Pass access which is included in some of the more expensive on-site resorts in not included here, neither is boat access to the theme parks or CityWalk.

ON-SITE TRANSPORTATION

At the Preferred and Premier level hotels, your transportation options to each the theme park include: shuttle buses, water taxis, rickshaws and walking paths. We do not recommend the shuttle buses as you won't save time as the drop-off point is a 10-minute walk from the theme parks.

The water taxis are our preferred form of transportation here, or simply walking. Water taxis begin operating from the hotels 30 minutes before Early Park Admission. The last departure from *CityWalk* is at 2:30am year-round.

The rickshaws are the quickest and most direct way to get around. These are approved by Universal and man-powered and have no set fee, simply tip what you think is appropriate ($2-$4 per person is customary).

At *Cabana Bay* and *Aventura Hotel* you can use the walking path or shuttle buses. The buses drop you off a 10-minute walk from the parks; the walking path route takes 20 to 25 minutes.

Shuttle buses run every 10 to 15 minutes to all hotels and are even more frequent to *the* Prime Value hotels.

Cabana Bay Beach Resort

This 2200-room, Retro-1950s and 1960s Prime Value hotel is one of the most affordable on-site options. There are walking paths to the parks and CityWalk (20 to 25 minutes) or you can use the complimentary shuttle.

Room size: Standard rooms are 300 ft^2, family suites are 430 ft^2 and 2-bedroom suites are 772 ft^2

Room prices: $129 to $214, plus tax for a standard room. Family suites are priced at $161 to $284, plus tax. 2-bedroom suites start at $350.

Activities: A 10-lane bowling alley; arcade room; two resort pools – one with a water slide; s'mores fire pit; hot hub; poolside movies and activities; a store; and a fitness center.

We were astounded on our first visit to *Cabana Bay Beach Resort*. It is a very well themed resort in a 1950s and 1960s style, and it has a fun feeling about it. There are also a wealth of things to do at the most affordable on-site property.

You can easily spend several days just exploring all the amenities on offer, and despite the fact the hotel has almost 2,000 rooms, the amenities never felt overcrowded to us.

We like the two sizes of rooms, and feel that they are reasonably priced for the location and amenities you get.

Standard rooms sleep up to 4 guests, and family suites sleep up to 6.

Even though this resort is significantly cheaper than many others, every room includes all the amenities you would expect: an LCD TV, an in-room safe, a coffee maker, an iron and a hair-dryer.

Suites also include a kitchenette area with a microwave, mini-fridge and sink.

We were also particularly appreciative of all the power outlets in the standard rooms and suites, including a multitude of USB sockets!

The resort's Table Service restaurant is part of the bowling alley (more on this later), though you are a short shuttle bus journey away from *CityWalk,* or you can walk to one of the other on-site hotels if you desire something more upscale for dinner.

Other food options include a large food court with many options and food trucks outside. In-room pizza delivery is also available.

Perhaps the biggest surprise is the exceptional entertainment on offer: the 10-lane bowling alley is unheard of at any other hotel ($15 per game, shoe rental $4 per pair, and food is available).

Many other amenities that are more commonly found at higher-priced resorts are available here too - and they are all complimentary.

There are two pools at the resort. The main pool measuring in at 10,000 ft^2 has a water slide, and the smaller 8000 ft^2 pool has a sandy beach. Both pools offer accessible zero-entry ramps. The smaller pool even has a lazy river going around it spanning 700 feet.

Free poolside activities happen throughout the day, and there are even s'mores pits to use.

Self-service laundry is available for $3 per wash and $3 per dryer load.

Parking is $12 per night for self-parking, payable at check-in.

There are, however, a few downsides to this resort: guests staying at *Cabana Bay* do NOT receive complimentary Express

Passes like at some other on-site hotels; this is usually cited as one of the main reasons for staying on-site.

However, the price difference between this hotel and those that include Express Pass access is huge, so this is understandable. There is also no water taxi service to this hotel.

However, *Cabana Bay* guests still have the option of walking paths to the resort (up to 25 minutes' walk), as well as continuous, complimentary shuttle bus transportation.

Large families and groups who want to stay together even have the option of the large 2-bedroom suites.

Overall, for those on a budget, but wanting the benefits of staying on-site, Cabana Bay is the best option.

DINING:

Bayline Diner – Quick Service food court. Entrées are $6.60 to $9.80 for breakfast, and $6.30 to $13.65 for lunch and dinner.

Galaxy Bowl Restaurant – Table Service dining and Quick Service food available too. Open from Noon to 11:00pm. Entrées are $9 to $13.

Atomic Tonic – Poolside bar with drinks and limited snacks. Cocktails are $13.

The Hideaway Bar & Grill – Poolside Bar and grilled fare. Entrees $5 to $10. Cocktails are $13.

Swizzle Lounge – Bar. Cocktails are $9 to $13. Other drinks from $6.50.

Starbucks – Quick Service location. Sells drinks and snacks at standard prices. Expect to pay $4-$6 per item.

Loews Sapphire Fall Resort

This 1000-room, 83-suite, hotel is classified as part of the Preferred category. It features a Caribbean-inspired design.

Transport: Water taxis, pedicabs, walking paths (15 to 20 minutes) and shuttle buses.

Room size: Standard rooms are 364 ft², and suites start at 529 ft².

Room prices: $179 to $284, plus tax for a standard room.

Activities: A large pool, two white sand beaches, a hot tub, children's water play area with pop jets, and a water slide; fire pit for s'mores; complimentary fitness center including a dry sauna; arcade game room; and a Universal Store.

This relatively new on-site resort is a beautiful, tropical destination. It provides a step up from *Cabana Bay* in terms of amenities and theming.

The centerpiece of the resort is the 16,000ft² pool - the largest in Orlando - as well as the two sandy beaches, and water slide. Pool-side cabanas are available.

Standard rooms sleep up to five people – a roll-away bed is needed at $25 per night for the fifth person.

There is also a 115,000 square foot convention space for business travelers.

This hotel does not include Express Pass access, and guests do not receive priority seating at restaurants. Both perks are reserved for the more expensive hotels that follow.

The hotel does, however, offer complimentary water taxi services to CityWalk and the theme parks - usually a perk reserved for the more expensive on-site options.

DINING:

New Dutch Trading Co. – With ready to go meals, beverages, fresh-baked breads and homemade jams, this is the stop for provisions and supplies. Food is $9 to $12.

Strong Water Tavern – A wall of vintage rums, a ceviche bar and a patio overlooking the lagoon make Strong Water Tavern a unique watering hole. There are also daily rum tastings, making this lounge a destination. Drinks & tapas are $6 to $18 each.

Amatista Cookhouse – Caribbean cuisine prepared in an exhibition kitchen. Whether dining indoors or out, or in one of the private dining areas, guests will feel welcomed and relaxed in this inspiring restaurant. Entrees are $13 to $27.

Drhum Club Kantine – Pool bar serving a Tapas-style menu. Food is $10 to $23, drinks start from $7.

Loews Royal Pacific Resort

This 1000-room, Preferred category hotel is themed to a tropical paradise. A standard room is 335ft². Water taxis, pedicabs, walking paths and buses are available to the parks.

TOP TIP

Due to the location of the dock, it is generally quicker to walk from this resort to *Islands of Adventure* and *CityWalk* than to use the water taxi service. The water taxi, however, is much more relaxing.

Room prices: $244 to $424 per night, plus tax
Activities: One very large pool, volleyball court, kids' water play area, fitness center, croquet, poolside activities, a torch lighting ceremony, and Wantilan Luau dinner show.

From the moment you step inside, you are a world away from the hustle and bustle of Orlando's theme parks. Yet, they are conveniently located right next door.

There is one large pool at this hotel, a complimentary gymnasium with a variety of cardio and free weight equipment, as well as steam and sauna facilities and a whirlpool.

An on-site coin-operated laundry is also available.

'Dive-In movies' are screened by the pool on select nights, and pool-side cabanas are available from $100 per day.

On Friday and Saturday nights (and Tuesdays during the peak summer season) guests can enjoy the 'Torch Lighting Ceremony' with hula dancers and fire jugglers by the pool. There is no charge to watch this.

The hotel's laid back Polynesian vibe and its location make it a solid choice - this hotel includes unlimited complimentary Express Pass access for guests.

DINING:

Orchid Court Lounge and Sushi Bar – Snacks are $8 to $18. Sushi and sashimi starts at $6 and ranges to $120.
Islands Dining Room – Table Service. Breakfast is either a buffet or a la Carte. The buffet is priced at $19.50 per adult and $10 per child. All day entrées are $12 to $32.
Jake's American Bar – Bar, with light snacks and larger meals. Entrées are $13 to $35.
Bula Bar and Grille – Poolside bar and dining. Entrées are $11 to $17.
Emeril's Tchoup Chop – Signature Table Service. Entrées are $12 to $18 at lunch, and $24 to $36 at dinner.
Wantilan Luau – Hawaiian dinner show starting at 5:00pm or 6:00pm on Saturdays (and also Tuesdays during peak season). Reservations required. Buffet including non-alcoholic and select alcoholic drinks; priced at $69 to $76 for adults, and $35 to $40 for children.

Hard Rock Hotel Orlando

This rock 'n' roll, Premier tier, hotel has a mere 650 rooms, including 33 suites. It is the second most expensive hotel on-site, and the closest to the parks.

TOP TIP

The plaques next to musical memorabilia in the hotel each have a unique number on them. Call (407) 503-2233 and enter the number on the plaque to learn about the item you are looking at.

Transport: Water taxis, pedicabs, walking paths (5 mins to *USF* and 10 mins to *IOA*) and shuttle buses.
Room size: 375 ft² for a standard room
Room prices: $289 to $494 per night, plus tax
Activities: Pool, Jacuzzis, poolside movies, volleyball court, and a fitness center.

Feel like rock 'n' roll royalty at the *Hard Rock Hotel* - lively, yet laid back.

The highlight of the hotel is the huge 12,000ft² zero-entry, white sand pool. It even has an underwater sound system and a slide!

The area also has a beach with a volleyball court and lounge chairs. There are two Jacuzzis, including one for adults only.

Most nights there is a poolside 'dive-in movie', and sometimes even dive-in concerts.

Poolside bar orders are available. Cabanas cost $80 to $200 per day, with soft drinks, bottled water, a TV, fresh fruit, towels and a refrigerator.

DJ lessons are held daily in the lobby in peak season, and you can even rent out a *Fender by AXE* guitar at no extra cost during your stay, with a $1000 refundable deposit.

This hotel is the closest to *CityWalk* and the theme parks, and is right next door to *Universal Studios Florida*. This makes a midday dip in the pool a real possibility.

Velvet Sessions – The Ultimate Cocktail Party: From January to October, on the last Thursday of each month, you can enjoy *Velvet Sessions* at the hotel's Velvet Bar. Each Session showcases a different type of beverage to taste along with great live rock music.

Tickets are $29 in advance from www.velvetsessions.com or $35 on the door.

DINING:

The Palm Restaurant – Table Service dining, steakhouse. Entrées are $13 to $59.
Velvet Bar – Bar with light snacks and bigger plates too. Entrées are $14 to $26.
The Kitchen – Buffet breakfast. Table Service at lunch & dinner. Entrées are $12 to $37.
Emack & Bolio's – Ice cream, pizzas and small bites. Entrées are $9 to $23.
BeachClub – Bar and Quick Service snacks. Snacks are $7 to $18.
Reservations for Table Service dining establishments can be made at OpenTable.com

Loews Portofino Bay Hotel

Portofino Bay is the best example of what a Premier level luxury resort should be. This 750-room hotel is incredibly well-themed to a small Italian fishing village.

In the evenings, weather permitting, the hotel has live music and classical singers, and guests can enjoy the atmosphere.

At **Family Art Photography** you can get a complimentary family photo-shoot. Sessions last 15 to 30 minutes. Prints start at $30 each. A DVD of your entire shoot will set you back $375, plus tax.

Harbor Nights:
Four times per year, the Portofino Bay Resort hosts 'Harbor Nights', a wine tasting and jazz event designed to capture the ambiance of the Mediterranean. Each event features select wines, gourmet food, live music and other live entertainment.

Pricing is usually $45 per person in advance, or $55 on the door (subject to availability). VIP seating is $75. All prices exclude tax. There is even a Holiday edition with a tree-lighting ceremony.

Transport: Water taxis, pedicabs, walking paths and shuttle buses.
Room size: 450 ft² for a standard room
Room prices: $304 to $494 per night, plus tax
Activities: 3 pools, poolside movies, spa, live music.

This luxury hotel recreates the charm and romance of the seaside village of Portofino, Italy, right down to the streets and cafés.

The hotel has 3 pools - one with a waterslide, the other has a Jacuzzi area and the quiet Hillside Pool overlooks the Bay. Saturdays in peak season, there is a 'Dive-In Movie'. Pool cabanas are available from $75 per day.

The **Mandara Spa** offers a variety of indulgent experiences. A 50-minute massage starts at $130, and you can expect to pay up to $595 for a 6-hour experience. Facials, nail services, waxing and haircuts are also available. On-site guests get free fitness club access. A fitness day pass is available at $25 by non-hotel guests.

The walking path is a lovely 20-minute walk to the theme parks, though we recommend taking the water taxi to relax.

DINING:

Bice – Table Service gourmet dining. Entrées are $19 to $48.
The Thirsty Fish Bar – Bar with light snacks. Open from 6:00pm. Drinks from $6.50.
Trattoria del Porto – Table Service dining. Entrées are $9 to $18 at breakfast, and $10 to $34 for lunch and dinner. A 'make your own pasta' meal is $26 for adults and $12 for kids.
Mama Della's Ristorante – Family style Italian cuisine. Mains are $20 to $38.
Sal's Market Deli – Quick Service. Sandwiches, paninis and pizzas. Pizzas are $14 to $18.
Gelateria Caffe Espresso – Coffees, pastries and ice creams priced at $3 to $7.50.
Bar American – Upscale bar. Open from 5:00pm to midnight. Food is $12 to $16.
Splendido Pizzeria – Pizza, salads and sandwiches. Entrées are $12 to $16. Cocktails - $13.
Reservations for Table Service dining establishments can be made at OpenTable.com

Universal Studios Florida

Universal Studios Florida opened in 1990 as the Floridian cousin to the popular Universal Studios theme park in Hollywood. The original idea of the park was to experience how movies were made. Actual filming would be done in the park too.

Over the years, the focus of the park has changed slightly and the philosophy is now to ride and "experience the movies" for yourself, rather than seeing how they are made. The park hosted just under 10 million guests in 2016.

Note: Average attraction waits noted in this section here are estimates for busy summer days during school break. Wait times may well be lower at other times of the year. They may also occasionally be higher, especially during the week of 4th July, Thanksgiving, Christmas, New Year and other public holidays.

Where we list food prices, this information was accurate during our last visit to the restaurant. We include a sample of the food on offer and not the full menu. Meal prices listed do not include a drink, unless otherwise stated. When an attraction is listed as requiring lockers, all loose items must be stored in complimentary locker storage outside the attraction.

Attraction Key

In the next two chapters, we list each attraction individually along with some key information. Here are what the symbols in the next sections mean.

	Does it have Express Pass?		Minimum height (in inches)
	Is there an On-Ride Photo?		Ride/Show Length
	Average wait times (on peak days)		
	Do I need to place my belongings in a locker before riding?		

Production Central

Production Central is the gateway to Universal Studios Florida. You pass through it to get to the rest of the park; it contains shops and a number of attractions.

Production Central is home to **Guest Services** where you can request disability passes, make dining reservations, ask questions, provide positive feedback and make complaints. You can also exchange some currencies at this location. Guest service is located to the right after the turnstiles.

To the left of the turnstiles you will find **lockers**, as well as **stroller** and **wheelchair rentals**.

The **Studio Audience Center** (to the right after the turnstiles) is the place to get tickets for shows being filmed in the soundstages at Universal. Tickets are complimentary. This is also the location for **Lost and Found**.

First Aid is located next to the Studio Audience Center. Another First Aid station is located next to Louie's Italian Restaurant.

You will also find the **American Express Passholder Lounge** in this area of the park, opposite the Shrek shop. This lounge is reserved for those who use an AmEx card to buy park tickets or an annual pass directly from Universal.

Inside the lounge you will find bottled water, snacks and phone charging facilities. Simply show your ticket receipt, the ticket itself, and your AmEx card for entry. Guests who use

an AmEx card for in-park purchases but do not use it to purchase their park tickets, do not have access to this lounge.

If you need to mail something, you can drop off your letters and postcards at the **mailbox**, located to the left as you come in after the turnstiles, to the right of the lockers.

Stamps can be bought from the On Location shop here on the Front Lot. **Calling cards** can be bought from a vending machine near the **lockers**.

Family & Health Services, which includes a nursing room, is located to the right after the turnstiles.

Attractions

Despicable Me: Minion Mayhem

	Yes		40"		No		4 minutes		No		60 to 120 minutes

A simulator ride featuring 4D effects and the characters from *Despicable Me*.

Due to the low hourly capacity and the popularity of its characters, queues are almost always lengthy.

Top Tip: A stationary version of this attraction operates with benches at the front of the theater. These do not move, but you get the 3D experience. When this is offered, the wait time is usually short, e.g. 10 minutes versus 90 minutes.

There is a separate queue line for this.

Fun Fact: The trees outside the ride are banana trees, as the minions love the yellow fruit!

Shrek 4-D

	Yes		None		No		12 minutes		No		15 to 45 minutes

Stepping into *Shrek 4D*, you know you are getting into a different kind of attraction – it is not just a 3D, but a 4D experience.

The unique part of this attraction is the seats, which act like personal simulators. For those not wishing to experience the seat movement, a limited number of stationary seats are also available.

The movie is great fun with some corny jokes and jabs at Disney thrown in.

Hollywood Rip Ride Rockit

🎟 Yes	51"-79"	📷 Yes	✓ 2 minutes	🔒 Yes	⏳ 45 to 90 minutes

Hollywood Rip Ride Rockit is a unique roller coaster that dominates the skyline from the distance even before you step foot inside the park.

Once on-board, prepare to be held in by just a lap bar-style restraint as you start your vertical climb to the top for your musical thrill adventure.

On this ride, you get to choose from a pre-selected number of songs to play during your ride. Your choice of music will pump into your ears through individual seat speakers as your adrenaline races.

Disney fans can think of this as *Rock 'n' Roller coaster* but with more music choices, without the loops and much bigger drops.

Straight after the first drop, you enter a unique 'almost-a-loop' that is really fun; you do a loop but stay upright all the way round - a really unique experience.

Once the experience is over, in addition to on-ride photos, you can even purchase a music video of your ride filmed using on-board cameras and including your choice of song as the soundtrack!

A Single Rider line is available at this attraction.

Top Tip: Don't trust the Single Rider wait time that is posted at the attraction entrance - it is often exaggerated. We have often waited less than half of the official posted Single Rider wait time.

To help you estimate, in the Single Rider line, from the bottom of the stairs to being on the train is usually about 30 minutes.

Top Tip 2: As well as the songs displayed on the screen, there are many secret bonus songs that you can choose from. To access the secret song list, after closing your restraint, you will need to push and hold the ride logo on the screen for about 10 seconds. When you let go a number pad appears; type in a three-digit number for load the song.

A full list of the songs is available online with a quick search.

TRANSFORMERS: The Ride-3D

Yes	40"	No	4 minutes	No	90 to 150 minutes	

TRANSFORMERS is a 3D screen-based moving dark ride, similar to *The Amazing Adventures of Spider-Man* at *Universal's Islands of Adventure*.

The storyline follows the Autobots (good guys) protecting the AllSpark from the Decepticons (bad guys).

Your ride vehicle moves from set to set, acting as a moving simulator immersing you in the action.

TRANSFORMERS: The Ride will be doubly impressive to fans of the movie franchise, though those who have not seen them are still likely to enjoy the action-packed experience.

Our only issue with the ride is its similarity to the *Spider-Man* attraction in the theme park next door. Considering *Spider-Man* is over 15 years old, it feels like almost no technological or storytelling progress has been made since then. Plus, we have a personal penchant for the *Spider-Man* characters.

This ride often has one of the longest waits in the park, so try to get here early in the day or towards the end, when crowds are at their lightest.

A Single Rider line is also available - we have found that it typically reduces your wait to about half of the regular standby line or less.

An engineering masterpiece:
Ever wondered how such a long ride is packed into such a small building?

Universal's engineers came up with an ingenious way to reduce the ride's overall footprint: during the ride, while you are watching a scene on one of the giant screens, you and your vehicle are taken in an elevator up one floor that houses more of the ride.

Here the ride continues its course and you later come back down to the first floor via another elevator while you watch another giant screen – this is all done seamlessly and really is an incredible feat.

DINING

Universal Studios' Classic Monster Cafe – Quick Service. Accepts Universal Dining Plan. Serves chicken, lasagne, cheeseburgers, pizza and other fast-food style meals. Entrées are $9 to $17.

New York

This area of the park is themed around the big apple.

Attractions

Revenge of The Mummy

EX Yes	48"	📷 Yes	✓ 4 minutes	🔒 Yes	⧗ 20 to 60 minutes

A unique roller coaster featuring fire, smoke, forward and backwards motion, and more.

Revenge of The Mummy is one of the most fun coasters we have been on, starting off as a slow moving dark ride and then turning into a traditional roller coaster themed to the world of *The Mummy*.

Although the ride does not go upside down, and is not exactly the fastest attraction in Orlando, it does tell its story very well and really immerses you in the atmosphere. It is a great thrill, with surprises throughout.

The queue line is also incredibly detailed and contains several interactive elements. For example, while watching guests in another location on a screen, you can press a scarab beetle and the guests will feel a quick blast of air from underneath them, guaranteed to give them a fright.

But beware where you put your hands while waiting in line, as the treasure you see around you may not be all you think it is, and you might just be in for a surprise or two.

A Single Rider queue line is available. We recommend first-timers see the regular standby line once before using the Single Rider queue.

Fun Fact: *Revenge of the Mummy* replaced *Kongfrontation* (a ride based on King Kong), that was previously housed in the same building; a statue of the great ape has been left behind as a tribute in the treasure room. See if you can spot it!

The Blues Brothers Show

See Jake and Elwood, the Blues Brothers, take to the stage in this show.

Unlike other shows where you sit in a show-style amphitheater, *The Blues Brothers Show* takes place on a small stage in a street with more of a street-performer feel to it.

Crowds are not very big and most people just walk in and out during the show and it is worth stopping by.

Rock climbing

Next to *Revenge of the Mummy*, there is a small alleyway that has a 50-foot tall rock-climbing wall.

Climb it and once you reach the top, ring the bell to claim victory!

Race Through New York Starring Jimmy Fallon

| | EX) | Yes | | 40" | 📷 | No | ✓ | 25 minutes | 🔒 | No | ⏳ | None |

Opened in 2017, this is a 3D simulated adventure with Jimmy Fallon.

There is no standard queue line per se - you visit the kiosks next to the attraction or use the Universal Orlando app to obtain a return time on the day.

Once inside "NBC's Studios", you will be given a colored ticket and can then explore the first room. Here you will find NBC and Tonight Show memorabilia and clips from the show's 60+ year history.

Once your color is called, you can enter a second space with interactive games, more video clips and live performances. There are also seating areas. Finally, once your color is called again you collect your 3D glasses.

These waiting rooms are great fun and much better than standing in a standard line. You will wait about 15-20 minutes from entering the building before riding - the show's about 4 minutes.

Then you board the world's first "flying theater" where Jimmy will you "to a white-knuckle race." Prepare to "speed through the streets and skies of The Big Apple, encountering everything from iconic landmarks to the deepest subway tunnels and anything else that comes to Jimmy's mind."

DINING

Finnegan's Bar and Grill – Table Service. Accepts Universal Dining Plan. Serves salads, sandwiches, fish and chips, chicken, corned beef, sirloin steak and more. Entrées are priced at $11 to $22. This is our favorite place to eat in this theme park outside of Diagon Alley.
Louie's Italian Restaurant – Quick Service. Accepts Universal Dining Plan. Serves spaghetti and meatballs, pizza slices, whole pizza pies and fettuccine alfredo. Entrées are priced at $7.50 to $14. Whole pizza pies are priced between $32 and $35.
Starbucks and **Ben & Jerry's**– Quick Service/Snacks. Food and drinks are $3 to $6 each.

World Expo

World Expo is home to both a MEN IN BLACK attraction, as well as a Simpsons area. Fear Factor: LIVE is the live show in this area.

Attractions

MEN IN BLACK: Alien Attack

	Yes		42"		Yes		5 minutes		Yes		Less than 45 minutes

At *Men In Black*, your mission is to protect the city and defeat the attacking aliens.

You are sent in teams of 6 in vehicles and, using handheld laser guns, compete against another team of riders to defeat the aliens and get a high-score.

This ride is a fun, family-friendly experience that we highly recommend. A Single Rider line is available.

Top Tip: Hold down the trigger throughout the ride. You get points for doing this, regardless of whether you hit any targets or not.

Top Tip 2: For major points, shoot Frank the Pug who is hidden on the ride in the newspaper stand on the right side of the second room.

Fear Factor Live

 Yes None No  20 minutes No 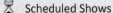 Scheduled Shows

Get ready to watch theme park guests face their fears live on stage as they compete against each other in *Fear Factor Live*. This is a fun show that unites the crowds together.

Alternatively, why not apply and be one of those guests? To participate in the show,

you will want to be near the entrance 60 to 90 minutes before show time. Guests must be over 18, have photo ID on them and be in good physical condition to participate.

Volunteers are also chosen to play minor roles during the show.

This show is starting to show its age, in our opinion, and we expect it to be replaced in the coming years by a new Harry Potter attraction, but for the moment it's a fun distraction - especially if you have never seen it before.

The Simpsons Ride

🎟 Yes	📏 40"	📷 No	✓ 6 minutes	🔒 No	⏳ 20 to 40 minutes

The Simpsons Ride brings the famous yellow Springfield family to life in a fun-filled simulator-style ride in front of an enormous screen - in this experience you enter Krustyland and ride a wild simulated roller coaster.

Your adventure is filled with gags throughout and is a fun family experience. Simpsons fans will love this ride!

Fun fact: During the pre-show video, look out for the DeLorean car and Doc Brown from Back to the Future. This is a tribute to the *Back to the Future* attraction that previously occupied the same building.

Kang and Kodos' Twirl 'N' Hurl

This is a fairly standard fairground-style spinning ride, like Disney's *Dumbo* attraction.

Here, you sit in flying saucers and spin around. A lever allows you to control the height of your saucer.

Around the attraction there are pictures of Simpsons characters; when you fly past them, they speak.

This attraction features Express Pass, though waits are usually under 10 minutes.

The Springfield Area: There are many photo opportunities here, including a giant Lard Lad donut sculpture, Chief Wiggum by his police car, a statue of Jebediah Springfield, Duff Man flexing his muscles and more. Characters often meet in this area, and there are carnival games you can pay to play.

DINING

Fast Food Boulevard – Quick Service. Accepts Universal Dining Plan. From the outside, it looks like several separate Simpsons buildings. Inside, it is actually one area with the following sections:
- **Moe's Tavern** sells Buzz Cola, Flaming Moes and Duff Beer ($3 to $8)
- **Lisa's Teahouse of Horror** sells salads and wraps ($6 to $10)
- **Luigi's** sells personal-sized pizzas ($10)
- **The Frying Dutchman** sells fish ($10 to $16)
- **Cletus' Chicken Shack** sells fried chicken and chicken sandwiches ($8 to $11)
- **Krusty Burger** sells burgers and hot dogs ($9.50 to $15.50)

Duff Brewery – Bar with snacks. Drinks are $3-$8, a hot dog is $8 and chips are $2.80.
Bumblebee Man's Tacos – Quick Service. Drinks are $3 to $6.50, tacos are $7 to $9.

Hollywood

Hooray for Hollywood! This area of the park is under redevelopment - Terminator 2: 3D closed in late 2017 - this was a special effects show merging 3D with live actors. The attraction replacing it has not yet been announced - we do know it will be an "all-new live-action experience based on a high-energy Universal franchise," arriving sometime in 2019.

Attractions

Universal's Horror Make Up Show

Yes	None	Yes	25 minutes	No	Scheduled Shows

Go behind the scenes and see how gory and horror effects are created for Hollywood movies in this fun and educational show that is sure to have you in stitches.

The script is very well thought out, with laugh after laugh, and some fun audience interaction too. This is one show we highly recommend you visit!

The theatre is relatively small so do get there early.

If you want to be part of the show, the hosts tend to choose young women in the middle section of the theatre. They also tend to go for someone who they think will speak no English, for comedic effect.

DINING

Mel's Drive In – Quick Service. Serves cheeseburgers and root beer floats. Accepts Universal Dining Plan. Entrées are $9.50 to $12.

Beverly Hills Boulangerie – Quick Service. Accepts Universal Dining Plan. Serves sandwiches, pastries, cakes, soups and salads. Entrées are $9 to $10.

San Francisco

This area of the park has changed immensely over the years, especially the opening of The Wizarding World of Harry Potter: Diagon Alley a few years ago. Now, San Francisco is once again going through a major redevelopment. A brand new ride – Fast & Furious: Supercharged – will open in 2018.

Attractions

Fast & Furious: Supercharged

In 2018, the San Francisco area of the park will welcome a new attraction.

Universal says that the *Fast & Furious* attraction will "fuse everything you love about the films with an original storyline and incredible ride technology."

"You'll get to check out some of the high-speed, supercharged cars you've seen on the big screen. You'll be immersed in the underground racing world made famous in the films and explore the headquarters of Toretto and his team. Then, you'll board

specially-designed vehicles for an adrenaline-pumping ride with your favorite stars from the films."

Expect a race on big screens and simulator-style action. There will be a virtual line experience just like the Jimmy Fallon attraction.

DINING

Richter's Burger Co. – Quick Service. Accepts Universal Dining Plan. Serves burgers, salads, and chicken sandwiches. Entrées are priced at $9.50 to $12.
Lombard's Seafood Grille – Table Service. Accepts Universal Dining Plan. Serves salads, sandwiches, catch of the day, sirloin steak, stir-fry and more. Entrées are priced at $12 to $22.
San Francisco Pastry Company – Snacks and Quick Service. Serves sandwiches and pastries. Accepts Universal Dining Plan. Entrées are priced at $3 to $10.

Woody Woodpecker's Kid Zone

This is the area of the park dedicated to the younger members of the family. As you will see, Universal isn't just for adrenaline junkies.

Attractions

E.T. Adventure

	Yes		34"		No		5 minutes		No		Less than 20 minutes

A cute, if ageing, ride where you sit on bicycles, like in the E.T. movie, and soar through the sky while trying to keep E.T. safe.

It is a fun little ride with a fairly high capacity and one of the few *Universal Studios Florida* attractions that remains from the park's opening day.

The ride system allows you to 'cycle through the air' and makes for a truly immersive experience.

If you do not like heights, avoid this attraction.

A Day in the Park with Barney

	Yes		None
	No		No
	15 minutes		
	Scheduled Shows		

Join Barney and his friends for a fun-filled show where little ones can sing along. After the show, there is a play area, and you can meet Barney.

Curious George Goes to Town

A water play area. Be sure to bring a change of clothes for the little ones.

Fievel's Playland

A play area for the little ones to let off some steam. There is quite a lot of water here, including a dinghy slide, so be sure to bring a change of clothes.

Animal Actors on Location

| 🎟️ Yes | 📏 None | 📷 No | ✓ 20 minutes | 🔒 No | ⏳ Scheduled Shows |

A behind the scenes look at how animals are taught to act in films – there is even some audience participation.

Animal fans will enjoy it but in our opinion, the show is lacklustre with a big reliance on video clips and a lack of flow.

It is a shame to see this show, especially when compared to a similar show at *Disney's Animal Kingdom Park* that only features birds – Disney's show has humor, a great storyline and a real wow factor. This one just doesn't.

We would advise giving this a miss unless you are a big animal fan.

Woody Woodpecker's Nuthouse Coaster

| 🎟️ Yes | 📏 36" | 📷 No | ✓ 44 seconds | 🔒 No | ⏳ Less than 30 minutes |

Think of *Woody Woodpecker's Nuthouse Coaster* as a kid's first coaster – a way to get them introduced into the world of coasters before trying something a bit more intense.

The ride is great fun for the little ones or just for those not wanting to jump on the likes of *The Incredible Hulk Coaster* just yet.

It is a short ride, but should be more than enough to please young thrill seekers.

The Wizarding World of Harry Potter: Diagon Alley

The Wizarding World of Harry Potter is one of the best known areas at Universal, and it is split between the two theme parks. The Hogsmeade area is in Islands of Adventure, and Diagon Alley is in Universal Studios Florida.

Diagon Alley is a high street in the Harry Potter universe. As it cannot be seen by Muggles (non-Wizards), it is hidden behind a recreation of London's Waterfront at *Universal Studios Florida*.

On the waterfront are façades of London landmarks. As well as the Statue of Eros, is the Knight Bus which features an interactive shrunken head experience as seen in the Prisoner of Azkaban film.

Visitors enter Diagon Alley through Leicester Square station and transition into the Wizarding World via brick walls and the help of some sound effects.

Shops

• **Quality Quidditch Supplies** – Sells apparel, hats and pendants, brooms, Golden Snitches, and Quaffles.

• **Weasleys' Wizard Weezes** – Sells prank items, toys, novelty items and magic tricks, such as *Extendable Ears* and *Decoy Detonators*.

• **Madam Malkin's** – Find Hogwarts school uniforms, with ties, robes, scarves, and more. Also sells jewelry themed to the four school houses.

• **Ollivander's** (show and shop) – See a short show in which a wand picks a wizard. Then, buy your own.

• **Wiseacre's Wizarding Equipment** – From hourglasses to compasses, and telescopes to binoculars.

• **Wands by Gregorovitch** – The legendary wand shop.

• **Shutterbuttons** – Get a personalized "moving picture" just like the Harry Potter newspapers for $49.95. Up to 4 people can take part in the experience. You are supplied with robes, but you must bring your own wand.

Dining

Fans of the boy wizard will definitely not go hungry in Diagon Alley:

• **Leaky Cauldron** – Quick Service. Accepts Universal Dining Plan. Serves English fare such as Banger's and Mash, Toad in the Hole, Fish and Chips and more. Breakfast entrees are $12 to $17. Lunch and dinner entrées are $9.50 to $20.

• **Florean Fortescue's Ice Cream** – Quick Service. Serves ice cream and other treats, as well as breakfast items and pastries in the morning. Does not accept the Universal Dining Plan.

Ice Cream Flavors include: Earl Grey and Lavender, Clotted Cream, Orange Marmalade, Butterbeer, and others. Ice creams are $5 to $13.

We highly recommend the Butterbeer ice cream – it is delicious.

Diagon Alley also includes shopfront façades that make for great photo ops, such as the offices of the Daily Prophet, Broomstix, Flourish and Blotts, etc.

Knockturn Alley

Running alongside Diagon Alley, is the darker *Knockturn Alley*, described as a "gloomy back street" by Universal. The shops and store fronts here are filled with items related to Dark Magic.

The flagship store here is *Borgin and Burkes*, which sells dark items such as Death Eater masks, skulls and other sinister objects. Make sure to check out the vanishing cabinet.

This area is covered so it is always dark and creates a nighttime atmosphere. It is also very popular during Orlando's frequent rain showers.

Be sure to look out for the animated "Wanted" posters of the Death Eaters.

Check out the window with the tarantulas on it - though it may give you a bit more than you bargained for if you get too close.

There are also many interactive wand experiences available in this area (more on these later).

Two other streets in *Diagon Alley* have themed shop fronts and interactive wand touches – *Horizont Alley* and *Carkitt Market*.

Attractions

Harry Potter and the Escape from Gringotts

🎟 Yes	📏 42"	📷 Yes	✓ 5 minutes	🔒 Yes	⧗ 30 to 60 minutes

Outside Gringotts bank, marvel at the fire-breathing dragon on the roof. Then, head inside and prepare for the experience of a lifetime.

The queue line begins by going past animatronic Goblins hard at work in the grand marble lobby, followed by wizard vaults and a security area (where you have your photo taken). You even board a huge elevator while waiting.

Just like *Harry Potter and the Forbidden Journey* in *Islands of Adventure*, this attraction's queue line is as much of an experience as the ride itself. The storyline begins to unfold as you see signs of Harry, Ron and Hermione discussing their plans.

The ride itself is a "multidimensional" rollercoaster-type attraction. It mixes real world elements with 3D video on huge screens, much like *Forbidden Journey*.

There are drops and turns (but the ride never goes upside down) in the layout, and it is more a 3D-style ride than a roller coaster - more *Transformers* than *The Incredible Hulk*. The ride features 4K-high definition technology as well as 3D screens, with glasses being worn by riders.

Apart from one drop and a short high-speed section, this is not a hugely thrilling coaster. You are definitely there for the story and not huge thrills.

A Single Rider queue line is available, but it skips all the queue line scenes and leads directly to the loading area. The queue at this attraction is a significant part of the experience. However, if all you want is the ride itself, the Single Rider line can save you a significant amount of time.

Storyline – Spoiler Alert: The ride is inspired by the final film *Harry Potter and the Deathly Hallows – Part 2*, and a pivotal scene where Harry, Ron and Hermione break into Gringotts bank to steal a powerful Horcrux to help them defeat Lord Voldemort.

On *Harry Potter and the Escape from Gringotts*, you encounter the trio during this quest – but expect to meet some dangerous creatures and malicious villains as well! During the ride you will come face to face with Bellatrix Lestrange, security trolls, fire breathing dragons and even Voldemort himself.

Kings Cross Station and the Hogwarts Express

  Yes | None No 5 minutes No   15 to 60 minutes

At *Kings Cross Station*, guests can break through the wall onto Platform 9 ¾, and catch the *Hogwarts Express.* This real train ride will transport you through the countryside to *Hogsmeade Station* (located at *Universal's Islands of Adventure*).

The journey lasts about five minutes and, as you look out of train windows, you will see stories unfold – all on a full-sized train, with compartments to sit in just like Harry and his pals did in the movies.

During the journey, you may see Hagrid on his motorcycle, the English countryside, Buckbeak the Hippogriff, the purple Knightbus, the Weasley twins on brooms, and even some Dementors. There are many more surprises in store, of course, and not everything happens *outside* the train carriage.

Each of the *Hogwarts Express* trains seats 200 passengers, and the story in each direction is unique.

Once you hop off the train at *Hogsmeade*, you will be

able to explore the area and the Harry Potter themed attractions, including the incredible *Harry Potter and the Forbidden Journey* ride.

Important: In order to experience the *Hogwarts Express,* you must have a Park-to-Park ticket as you will physically move between theme parks. A Single-Park ticket does not allow you to experience this ride – guests with this ticket can experience each of the theme parks' Wizarding Worlds on separate days, but they cannot travel on the *Hogwarts Express*.

Ollivanders

 No | None No 3 minutes No Less than 10 minutes

Technically, this is a pre-show to a shop. You enter *Ollivanders* in groups of 25 people.

One person is chosen by the wand-master to find the right wand for them through the use of special effects. When the right one is found, they are given the opportunity to buy it in the

shop next door.

This is a fantastic experience that we highly recommend you visit. It is suitable for people of all ages.

The queue line at this *Ollivanders* moves much more quickly than the one in *Islands of Adventure*.

Interactive Wand Experiences

Interactive wand experiences are available at the *Wizarding World*, both at *Diagon Alley* and *Hogsmeade*.

In order to participate, guests must purchase an interactive wand from the *Wizarding World*'s shops. These are priced at $48; this is $8 more than the non-interactive wands.

Once you have purchased a wand, look for one of the 25+ bronze medallions embedded in the streets that mark locations you can cast spells. You also get a map of the locations included with each wand purchase.

Once standing on a medallion, perform the correct spell: draw the shape of the spell in the air with your wand and say the spell's name. Then, watch the magic happen.

This is a fun bit of extra entertainment, and wands can be reused on future visits.

Diagon Alley Live Entertainment

At *Carkitt Market*, two shows are performed daily:

The first show brings to life two fables from "The Tales of Beedle the Bard" – *The Fountain of Fair Fortune* and *The Tale of the Three Brothers*. This trunk show uses scenic pieces, props and puppetry.

The second show features a musical performance by *The Singing Sorceress: Celestina Warbeck and the Banshees*. With a whole lot of soul, this swinging show features songs including *A Cauldron Full Of Hot, Strong Love*, and *You Stole My Cauldron But You Can't Have My Heart*.

As well as the live stage shows, the area hosts many other interactive experiences.

Just outside Diagon Alley, you will find the *Knight Bus* and its two occupants: a shrunken head and the Knight Bus Conductor, who will be more than happy to chat, joke around and take photos with you.

Plus, at *Gringotts Money Exchange* you can exchange Muggle currency for Wizarding Bank Notes, which can be used throughout both Universal theme parks to purchase snacks and in stores.

Stores in *The Wizarding World* do accept regular US dollars and credit or debit cards, of course, but these Harry Potter bank notes can make for a cool souvenir.

Early Entry

Staying on-site at a Universal hotel entitles you to early admission into the *WWOHP* one hour before the general public.

This also applies to off-site hotels booked as part of a Universal vacation package online or through an authorized reseller – check this is included in your package.

Either *Diagon Alley* or *Hogsmeade* will be open. This changes regularly; check Universal's website to find out which one.

If you do not have early admission, be at the park entrance in advance; guests are often allowed in up to 30 minutes before the opening time.

Universal Studios Florida Park Entertainment

Universal Studios Florida is home to live entertainment throughout the day. Character meet and greets can be found throughout the park and there is a daily parade.

Universal's Superstar Parade

Expect to see The Minions and Gru from *Despicable Me*, Sponge Bob Squarepants, Dora the Explorer, characters from *The Secret Life of Pets* and many others in the daily *Universal Superstar Parade*.

This parade is great fun for character fans. Both the floats and the characters are great to see, and the upbeat music adds to the fun.

The parade route starts by *Universal's Horror Make Up Show*, moves towards the lagoon, past *TRANSFORMERS*, round the front of *Revenge of the Mummy*, down past the *Universal Stage* and *Despicable Me* and back along *Hollywood Boulevard* ending next to *Universal's Horror Make Up Show* where it started.

One of the best things about *Universal's Superstar Parade* is that it is much less crowded than the parades at Disney's theme parks.

Many people simply do not know it exists; and many go to Universal mainly for its thrill rides.

Having said this, although the parade is enjoyable, it is not up to the standards of a Disney parade. The parade is performed once each day; the time will be printed on your in-park map.

Top Tip: Twice per day, before the parade starts, there are dance parties hosted by Mel's Drive-In. During the dance parties, floats and characters from the parade come out to meet and greet, dance and sign autographs.

Please note that universal's nighttime show "Universal's Cinematic Spectacular: 100 Years of Movie Memories" is no longer performing as of November 2017, though it may be replaced with a new show in the future.

Universal's Islands of Adventure

Universal's Islands of Adventure opened in 1999 with many famed attractions such as *The Incredible Hulk Coaster* and *The Amazing Adventures of Spider-Man*, which instantly put it on the world theme park map.

The true revolution for the park, however, came with the opening of *The Wizarding World of Harry Potter: Hogsmeade* in 2010.

Expansion and innovation in the park have not stopped since the *Wizarding World* was unveiled. In this theme park you will not find 'lands' or areas, but 'islands' instead. Together these islands make up *Universal's Islands of Adventure*.

The park hosted 9.3 million guests in 2016.

Live Entertainment at the Park:
Unlike *Universal Studios Florida* next door, here there are no daily fireworks shows or parades.

There are, however, character appearances throughout the various lands, in particular in *Seuss Landing* and *Marvel Superhero Island*. There are no Harry Potter characters in *Hogsmeade*, except for the Hogwarts Express Conductor.

Port of Entry

Perhaps the most beautiful entrance to a theme park in Orlando, Port of Entry transports you to a different time and place.

There are no attractions in this area of the park. Instead, it acts as an entranceway to the Islands of Adventure themselves.

You will find many shops and a few places to eat in this area.

To the right of the welcome arch at Port of Entry, you will find **Guest Services**. Here, you can get help with accessibility, dining reservations, as well as questions, positive feedback and complaints. **Lost and Found** is also located here.

Lockers, a phone card vending machine and a **payphone** are all located to the left of the archway.

Strollers and **wheelchair rentals** can also be found here. **First Aid** is located inside the Open Arms Hotel building to the right of the entrance archway. There is another First Aid station in *The Lost Continent* by the bazaar.

Fun fact: At the wheelchair and stroller rental place look out for a sign listing the prices of rentals along with several gag items, which have already been "rented out" including a gondola, an aero boat and a rocket car.

DINING

Confisco Grille and Backwater Bar – Table Service. Accepts Universal Dining Plan. Serves wood-oven pizzas, sandwiches, pasta and fajitas. Entrées are $9 to $22.
Croissant Moon Bakery – Quick Service. Accepts Universal Dining Plan. Serves continental breakfasts, sandwiches, paninis, cakes and branded coffee. Entrées are $2.50 to $12.50. Note: This location is not listed on the map – it is on the right hand side of Port of Entry.
Starbucks – Quick Service. Drinks $2.50 to $5.20. Accepts Universal Dining Plan.

Seuss Landing

This area is themed to the Dr. Seuss books. To make this land look unique, the theme park designers even made sure there were no straight lines anywhere.

Attractions

One Fish, Two Fish, Red Fish, Blue Fish

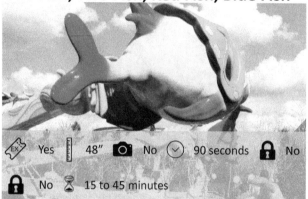

EX: Yes | 48" | 📷 No | ⌄ 90 seconds | 🔒 No

🔒 No | ⏳ 15 to 45 minutes

A classic spinning ride, like *Dumbo* in the Disney parks. This one, however, packs a bit of a twist.

The soundtrack is actually a set of instructions you should follow to stay dry. So when you hear "up, up, up" you will want to steer yourself upwards and be as high as possible to avoid a soaking. This is a fun twist on what can be a bit of an unimaginative type of ride. At colder times the water is turned off.

Children under 48" (1.22m) must ride with an adult.

Caro-Seuss-el

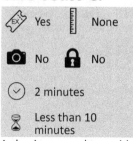

EX: Yes | None

📷 No | 🔒 No

⌄ 2 minutes

⏳ Less than 10 minutes

A classic carousel type ride themed to the Seuss series of books.

There is unlikely to be a wait for this ride at any time.

The High in the Sky Seuss Trolley Train Ride

EX: Yes | 40"

📷 Yes | 🔒 No

⌄ 5 minutes

⏳ 15 to 45 minutes

A cute, slow journey across the rooftops in Seuss Landing.

The minimum height is 40" (1.02m) to ride accompanied, or 48" (1.22m) to ride alone.

The Cat in the Hat

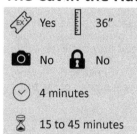

EX: Yes | 36"

📷 No | 🔒 No

⌄ 4 minutes

⏳ 15 to 45 minutes

Spin through the story of *The Cat in the Hat*. The ride makes more sense if you have read the books or seen the movies, but it is enjoyable for everyone.

DINING

Circus McGurkus Cafe Stoo-pendous – Quick Service. Accepts Universal Dining Plan. Serves pizza, pasta, salads, cheeseburgers and chicken. Entrées are priced at $9 to $15.

The Lost Continent

Themed to mythological creatures; home to acclaimed restaurant Mythos.

Attractions

Poseidon's Fury

Yes	None	No	15 minutes	No	15 to 45 minutes

A combination of a live show and walk-through experience with cool fire and water effects. Note that this show is standing room only.

In our opinion, this is a good watch but not worth more than a 30-minute wait. Return later in the day if wait is long.

The Eighth Voyage of Sindbad Stunt Show

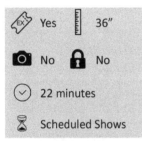

Yes   36"

No   No

22 minutes

Scheduled Shows

An action-packed show filled with special effects. These effects, however, are the problem: the show is just a montage of effects without a storyline.

If you are an action fan, watch it; if not, skip it.

The Mystic Fountain

A witty, talking, interactive fountain in a courtyard area. You can ask the fountain questions and have a chat.

The fountain also loves to tell jokes and to get people wet if they come too close!

The fountain only operates at select times of the day.

DINING

Mythos Restaurant – Table Service. Accepts Universal Dining Plan. Serves sandwiches, short-ribs, salmon and mahi mahi. Entrées are $13 to $23. This is our favorite in-park restaurant. It is only open for lunch.
Fire Eater's Grill – Quick Service. Accepts Universal Dining Plan. Serves hot dogs, chicken fingers and salads. Entrées are $9 to $12. Large portions.

Fun Fact: Stand under the bridge behind Mythos Restaurant to hear a troll.

The Wizarding World of Harry Potter: Hogsmeade

Step into the world of Harry Potter and experience a visit to Hogsmeade. Dine, shop and experience the wild rides. The area is incredibly themed and Potter fans will see authenticity unlike anywhere else. For guests who have previously visit, please note that the Dragon Challenge roller coaster closed in 2017.

Attractions

Harry Potter and the Forbidden Journey

A truly ground-breaking ride featuring projections, flexible ride vehicles and an incredibly detailed queue.

The opening of this attraction was a turning point in Universal Orlando's history, cementing its spot as one of the world's best theme park resorts.

The queue line of this attraction is an attraction unto itself, as you wind your way through Hogwarts castle watching specially crafted scenes and experience moments like the famous trio in the Potter books and movies.

At the end of the queue, it is time for an incredible adventure - this is a simulator-style attraction that blurs the lines between physical sets and on-screen projections. Plus, the moment your enchanted bench first takes off is

Yes   48"   Yes   5 mins   Yes   30 to 60 mins

breathtaking.

Expect to encounter dementors, take part in a quidditch match, come face to face with dragons and much more.

There is a Single Rider queue line available, which can cut down wait times significantly; waits are usually about 50-75% shorter than the standard wait time in our experience but this varies.

Warning: We feel this ride creates mental strain due to the simulated sensations and the screens in front of you. This means that if you ride it more than once back-to-back, you are likely to feel unwell.

Hidden Secret: When you are in Dumbledore's office hearing his speech, take a look at the books on the wall to the right of him. One of the books may do something very magical.

Hogsmeade Station and the Hogwarts Express

Catch the *Hogwarts Express*, and be transported through the countryside to *Kings Cross Station* (at *Universal Studios Florida*). The journey lasts several minutes and as you look out of the windows, you will see stories unfold.

Once you hop off the train at *Kings Cross* you will be by the London waterfront. There, you can enter Diagon Alley for its attractions, including *Harry Potter and the Escape from Gringotts*.

Important: Guests must

⮝ EXP	Yes	N/A	📷 No	✓	5 mins	🔒 No	⏳ 15 to 60 mins

have a Park-to-Park ticket to ride this attraction. Single Park tickets do not allow entry.

Flight of the Hippogriff

A small roller coaster where you soar on a Hippogriff and go past Hagrid's hut. Good family fun and a good starter coaster before putting your children on the likes of *The Hulk*.

Shops

The shops are as much of the experience as the rides. Be sure to step inside.
• **Filch's Emporium of Confiscated Goods** – The exit shop of *Forbidden Journey*. Sells apparel, mugs, photo frames, dark magic items and trinkets.

• **Honeydukes** – Those with a sweet tooth will find love potion sweets, chocolate frogs (with collectable trading cards) and more.
• **The Owlery and Dervish & Banges** – Sells wands, Horcrux replicas, clothing, stationery and even a model

of the Hogwarts Express.
• **The Owl Post** – A real post office where letters or postcards can be sent to friends and family with a Hogsmeade postmark and stamp. Stationery on sale.

Restaurants

The restaurants in Hogsmeade are well-themed and the Quick Service food is some of the best in the park. We recommend you take a look inside these, even if you do not eat there.
• **Hog's Head** – Quick Service. No Universal Dining

Plan. This pub is located in the same building as *Three Broomsticks*. Serves alcoholic beer, non-alcoholic Butterbeer and juices. Drinks are $2.50 to $7.
• **Three Broomsticks** – Quick Service. Accepts Universal Dining Plan. Serves breakfast meals.

At lunch and dinner, you will find Cornish pasties, fish & chips, shepherd's pie, smoked turkey legs, rotisserie chicken and spareribs. Entrées are $9.50 to $17. Family platters for 4 people are available for $60.

Skull Island

Attractions

Skull Island: Reign of Kong

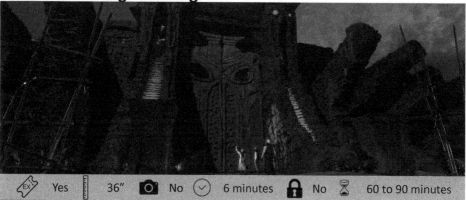

⬦ EX	Yes	📏 36"	📷 No	✓ 6 minutes	🔒 No	⏳ 60 to 90 minutes

The newest attraction at Universal's *Islands of Adventure* is *Skull Island: Reign of Kong*.

Step aboard one of the huge 72-seat 4x4 vehicles. Once on board each ride promises to be unique as one of five different drivers takes you on an adventure.

Universal puts it best: "You'll navigate perilous jungles, explore ancient temple structures, and encounter hostile natives – and that's only the beginning."

"Throughout the rest of your excursion, you'll brave foreboding caves crawling with prehistoric creatures, fend off unspeakable terrors – and even come face-to-face with the colossal Kong himself."

The animatronics, music and atmosphere created here are second to none and we expect *Reign of Kong* to remain one of the most popular attractions in the park for a while.

This is currently the newest attraction in the park. To minimise your wait, make this either the first attraction you visit during the day - or the last.

A Single Rider line is available - wait times here are usually about half of the regular queue line.

Top Tip: If you want to see Kong up close, sit on the right hand side of the vehicle - each side provides a different and unique experience. The drivers also change up the experience too.

Warning: The queue line for this ride is dark and there are actors in the queue line ("the natives") who scare guests as they wait. The ride may also be too intense for young children.

Jurassic Park

Since the Jurassic Park movie became a classic in 1993, children and adults alike have dreamed of visiting this magical world of dinosaurs. Universal's Islands of Adventure allows those dreams to come true.

Attractions

Jurassic Park River Adventure

On a boat, glide past huge dinosaurs. However, this calm river adventure soon changes course. Watch out for the T-Rex before your 85-foot drop! A Single Rider line is available at this attraction.

Top Tip: The back row gets you less wet.

Note: Lockers are optional and cost $4 for 90 minutes of locker time.

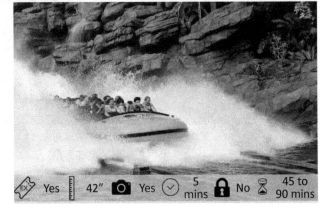

Yes   42"   Yes   5 mins   No   45 to 90 mins

Camp Jurassic

A play area themed to the Jurassic Park movies. We definitely recommend exploring the area, as the detail is just incredible.

This play area isn't only reserved for children. Anyone can explore the area, from the caves to the water jets and the treetop platforms to the slides.

Fun Fact: Step on the dinosaur footprints for a roaring sound.

Jurassic Park Discovery Center

An exploration area where you can see model dinosaurs, play dinosaur-themed carnival-style games, learn about DNA sequencing, and witness a dinosaur birth.

Top Tip: Exit out the back doors and you will find an outdoor patio area, which is a great place to take long-shot photos of *Islands of Adventure*.

Pteranodon Flyers

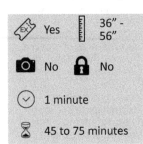

Yes   36" - 56"

No   No

1 minute

45 to 75 minutes

Soar above Jurassic Park on a winged dinosaur glider.

Guests over 56" must be accompanied by someone under 36" tall to ride.

DINING

The Burger Digs – Quick Service. Accepts Universal Dining Plan. Serves burgers, chicken tenders and chicken sandwiches. Entrées are $8 to $10.
Thunder Falls Terrace – Quick Service. Accepts Universal Dining Plan. Serves cheeseburgers, ribs, smoked turkey legs, wraps, and rotisserie chicken. Entrées are $13 to $16. The portion sizes are large.

Toon Lagoon

Toon Lagoon is an entire land dedicated to water – with two of the park's water attractions here, as well as water elements everywhere.

Attractions

Dudley Do-Right's Ripsaw Falls

Yes | 44" | Yes | 7 minutes | No | 45 to 75 minutes

Want a water ride that gets you absolutely soaked? Give this one a try.

The ride contains a well-themed interior and culminates in several drops with a final rollercoaster-style splashdown making sure you leave thoroughly drenched. The ride reaches a top speed of 45mph (over 70 km/h), so you get a great thrill! A Single Rider queue line is available at this attraction.

Optional lockers are available for a fee of $4 for 90 minutes.

Popeye & Bluto's Bilge-Rat Barges

Yes | 42"

No | No

6 minutes

45 to 90 minutes

Popeye's will make sure you come out drenched from head to toe. This is by far the wettest water ride at Universal and it is a whole lot of fun! Universal has come up with creative ways to wet you.

Optional lockers are available costing $4 for 90 minutes; the center of the raft has a covered section for basic water protection too.

Me Ship, The Olive

This is a kids play area and a great place for a break from the crowds.

For those who like causing chaos, there are free water cannons on the top level of the ship to spray guests on the Popeye water ride below.

DINING

Blondie's – Quick Service. Accepts Universal Dining Plan. Serves sandwiches, made to order subs and hot dogs. Entrées are $10 to $12.

Comic Strip Cafe – Quick Service. Accepts Universal Dining Plan. Serves Chinese beef and broccoli, chilidogs, sandwiches, fish & chips, pizza, and spaghetti and meatballs. Entrées are $9.50 to $14.

Wimpy's - Quick Service. Accepts Universal Dining Plan. Serves burgers at $10 to $12.

Marvel Super Hero Island

This island contains two of our favourite attractions in all of Universal Orlando – Spider-Man and The Hulk. There is also fun comic book theming, places to eat and shop, and other attractions. You will often find Marvel characters meeting guests in this area of the park.

Attractions

The Amazing Adventures of Spider-Man

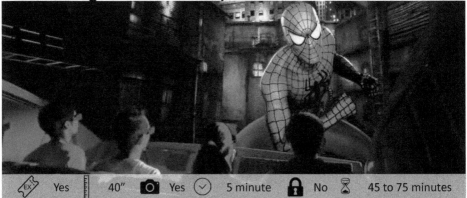

Yes	40"	Yes	5 minute	No	45 to 75 minutes

One of the most ground-breaking rides in the world, *The Amazing Adventures of Spider-Man* is a world-class attraction that incorporates projection screens with real world elements like never seen before.

More than a decade after its opening, the attraction has not aged a single bit, as it has been updated with 4K and 3D technology creating higher resolution images. The storyline works as well as it ever has.

The ride still wins awards and it sure is a fun experience swinging around New York City with Spider-Man. It is an absolute must-do.

This ride operates a Single Rider line, which can often save you a lot of time.

Doctor Doom's Fearfall

Yes	52"	No	45 seconds	No	45 to 60 minutes

Love drop towers? Then you will adore this ride.

Doctor Doom needs your screams for power; to get them, he shoots you up in the air – and he definitely gets more than enough power.

The ride consists of one high speed launch up, followed by a free-fall back down (and then up and down until you stop).

This attraction operates a Single Rider queue line – ask for it at the entrance.

Fun Fact: Look on the ground outside the attraction for chalk outlines of the Fantastic Four. They, too, went on the ride and came plummeting to the ground, landing where the outlines are. A subtle feature, but really cool.

The Incredible Hulk Coaster

| | EX⤙ Yes | 📏 54" | 📷 Yes | ✓ 2 minutes | 🔒 Yes | ⧖ 30 to 90 minutes |

Winner of numerous awards, *The Incredible Hulk Coaster* is our favorite roller coaster in all of Orlando.

It is a truly outstanding thrill with huge loops, an underground section, and non-stop fun from the moment you are launched out of the tunnel until you are back at the station.

There is a Single Rider line at this attraction; just ask the ride attendant at the front to use it – the waits are often short as it is not well signposted.

Storm Force Accelatron

| | EX⤙ Yes | 📏 48" | 📷 No | ✓ 1 minute | 🔒 No | ⧖ Less than 10 minutes |

A standard teacup style ride themed to Marvel super hero, Storm - and it's fast! An adult must accompany those under 48 inches (1.22m) tall.

DINING

Captain America Diner – Quick Service. Accepts Universal Dining Plan. Serves cheeseburgers, chicken sandwiches, chicken fingers and salads. Entrées are $9.50 to $12.50.
Cafe 4 – Quick Service. Accepts Universal Dining Plan. Serves pizza, pasta, sandwiches and salads. Entrées are $9 to $14. Whole pizza pies are $32 to $35.

Volcano Bay

Volcano Bay is Universal Orlando's newest major addition - a water park based around an enormous, 200-foot-tall volcano - Krakatau.

Transport

Universal Orlando is in a unique situation where it is landlocked on all four sides and therefore has to be creative about its use of land. As such, Volcano Bay is located on a small parcel of land next to Cabana Bay Beach Resort.

Volcano Bay does not have a parking lot and therefore guests staying off-site will need to park at the normal Universal parking garages as for the theme parks and catch a complimentary shuttle bus to Volcano Bay.

Guests of all six on-site hotels (except Cabana Bay) also have a complimentary shuttle bus from the hotel to the water park. Guests staying at Cabana Bay can simply walk to Volcano Bay as it is right next door.

TapuTapu

Universal has attempted to revolutionise the concept of a water park by creating a park free from queue lines.

To do this you will need a wearable band called a TapuTapu - it is similar to a Magicband at Disney, but with a screen. It is given to you for using during the day once you are inside Volcano Bay - you must return it when leaving the park.

The TapuTapu allows you to do several things:

• **TapTu Ride** - The attractions at Volcano Bay do not have standard queue lines. Instead, outside each attraction you will see a totem pole an a posted wait time. Tap your TapuTapu on the totem pole and you will be given a return time. Then, simply return to the ride entrance when your wristband vibrates to alert you. You will have to wait in a short queue to enter (usually 5-10 minutes, though at peak periods it could be up to 30 minutes).

You can only virtually queue for one attraction at a time.
• **TapTu Play** - Throughout the park you will find interactive elements - at these, you can tap your TapuTapu and special events will be triggered, such as a spray of water onto the lazy river or a pattern of lights appearing inside a cave.
• **TapTu Pay** - Using the Universal Orlando app, you can link your park tickets and TapuTapu to a payment card and then use your wearable to pay throughout

the day. You can also set spending limits and add a PIN when paying.
• **TapTu Snap** - Throughout the park there are framed photo spots, simply tap your TapuTapu and pose. On-ride photos can also be obtained using your wristband. All these photos will appear on the Universal Orlando app and you can buy full-quality versions there.
• **TapTu Lock** - Use your TapuTapu to unlock your park locker (extra charge) - you can assign up to 4 wristbands to one locker using the locker screen. There is an extra charge for locker use.

Lockers

There are four-in park locations to rent lockers at Volcano Bay: near Kohola Reef Restaurant, near Bambu, near Whakawaiwai Eats and next to Wautri Marketplace. Lockers come in three sizes from small to large, priced at $8, $12 and $15 for the day.

You can store and retrieve items from the lockers as many times as you would like throughout the day. You can pay with card, cash, your room key or your TapuTapu linked to a payment card. In all cases you will need a TapuTapu to access your locker.

Cabana and premium seating include use of a complimentary locker.

There are also lockers just outside Volcano Bay's entrance priced at $10 for the whole day. These are operated using a credit card and are no way near as convenient the in-park lockers. We would only recommend using these if there are no in-park lockers left.

Cabana Rentals and Premium Seating

To truly maximise your Volcano Bay experience why not take advantage of one of the premium upgrade options?

• **Premium Seating** - If you want to avoid having to search for a sun lounger, this is the perfect option. Premium Seating is a set of 2 sunloungers with a sun blocking shade, a locker and a shared server who takes food and drink orders. Pricing is $30 to $70 per day, depending on the season.
• **Cabana Rentals** - The ultimate in luxury, there are several different varieties of cabanas for you to choose from. All include: sun loungers, fridge with bottled water, complimentary fruit, cabana attendant and towels. The best feature, though, is a tablet which allows you to reserve your place in line for any of the park's rides from your cabana without having to physically tap your TapuTapu. A single cabana for up to 6 people is priced at $160 to $450 at the lower level and $200 to £550 on the raised level. A family suite for up to 16 people is $300 to $600.

Attractions

For each attraction we list minimum height requirements and maximum guests weight restrictions.

Krakatau:
At the heart of the park, you'll see the 200-foot-tall volcano called Krakatau. By day, you'll see its majestic waterfalls. And by night, the volcano illuminates with blazing lava.

Three body slides are found at the rear of the volcano, and each starts off with surprise doors that drop out from beneath you:
• *Ko'okiri Body Plunge*: (48", 300 lbs) A racing, 70-degree drop that plummets 125-feet through the center of Krakatau. It is the world's

first slide to travel through a pool filled with guests.

• *Kala and Ta Nui Serpentine Body Slides*: (48", 230 lbs) Two intertwining drop slides where you'll fall freely along 124 twisting feet. Green is more intense than blue.

• *Punga Racers*: (42", 49" to ride alone) A high-speed race through four different enclosed slides featuring manta-shaped mats.

• *Krakatau Aqua Coaster*: (42", 49" to ride alone, 700 lbs combined) The park's star attraction where you sit in canoes and travel both upwards and downwards through the park's iconic volcano. A 4-person water rollercoaster. Very fun.

Wave Village:
Located at the base of Krakatau, Wave Village is a perfect place to soak in the sun and relax on the sandy shores. It includes:

• *Waturi Beach*: (Under 48" must wear a life vest) A multi-directional wave pool where you can swim, relax on the sand or indulge in private, one- or two-story cabanas.

• *The Reef*: (Under 48" must wear a life vest) An adjacent leisure pool with calmer waters and views of riders on the Ko'okiri Body Plunge.

River Village:
River Village offers several family-friendly attractions and experiences and features:

• *Kopiko Wai Winding River*: (Under 48" must wear a life vest) A gentle, winding river that passes through the volcano's hidden caves, featuring spontaneous water effects and a journey through the cave of starlight.

• *Tot Tiki Reef*: (Max 48") A toddler play area with spraying Maori fountains, slides and a kid-size volcano.

• *Runamukka Reef*: (Max 48") A three-story water playground inspired by the coral reef with twisting slides, sprinklers and more.

• *Honu*: (48", 700 lbs combined) An adventurous, 2 to 5-passenger raft ride that soars across a dual wall.

• *Ika Moana*: (42", 49" to ride a lone, 800 lbs combined) A twisting, 2 to 5-passenger raft ride that glides across bubbling geysers.

Rainforest Village:
Features an incredible assortment of attractions for thrill-seekers, including:

• *Maku*: (42", 49" to ride alone, 1050 lbs combined) A "saucer ride" sending 2 to 6-passenger rafts speeding around three saucer-shaped curves.

• *Puihi*: (42", 49" to ride alone, 850 lbs combined) A 3 to 6-passenger raft ride that plunges you into darkness before bursting into a funnel and a zero-gravity drop.

• *Ohyah and Ohno Drop Slides*: (48") Two twisting, adrenaline-pumping slides that launch you four- or six-feet above the water at the end. Lifeguards will require to confirm you can swim as the end pool is 10ft deep.

• *TeAwa The Fearless River*: (42" with life vest, 49" to ride alone without life vest) An action-packed, racing torrent river where you'll have to hang tight in your inner tube amidst roaring, whitewater rapids.

• *Taniwha Tubes*: (42", 49" to ride alone, 300 lbs single or 450 lbs combined) Four unique Easter Island-inspired slides with rafts for single or double riders.

• *Puka Uli Lagoon*: (Under 48" must wear life vest) A tranquil pool where you can swim and relax.

Guests with Express Pass access can simply enter through the ride entrances without needing to use their TapuTapu to reserve a time. They must wait in the queue until it is their turn once entering each attraction.

DINING

Whakawaiwai Eats – Quick Service. Accepts Universal Dining Plan. Serves pizza, salads, hot dogs, and mac & cheese. Entrées are $7.50 to $12.

The Feasting Frog – Quick Service. Accepts Universal Dining Plan. Serves tacos, nachos and corn dogs. Entrees are $9 to $12.

Bambu – Quick Service. Accepts Universal Dining Plan. Serves burgers, salads and sandwiches. Entrees are $7.50 to $15.

Dancing Dragon's Boat Bar – Bar with drinks and snacks. Accepts Universal Dining Plan.

Kanuku Boat Bar – Bar with drinks and snacks. Does not accept Universal Dining Plan.

Kohola Reef Restaurant & Social Club – Quick Service. Accepts Universal Dining Plan. Serves fried chicken, burgers, pizzas, seafood, ribs and salads. Entrees are $10 to $17

CityWalk

CityWalk is located just outside the theme parks, and within walking distance of all the on-site hotels. There are shops, restaurants, bars, cinemas and clubs.

CityWalk is Universal Orlando's entertainment district, open from 11:00am to 2:00am daily - admission is free.

CityWalk is often compared to *Disney Springs*, but this location is much smaller. *CityWalk* also has more of an adult feel to it, particularly at nighttime, when there is a focus on the club-like atmosphere. The shops and dining locations are also much more limited. It still, however, manages to still keep a fun and friendly atmosphere no matter the time of day.

Parking is charged before 6:00pm at the main Universal parking garages used for the theme parks. After 6:00pm, parking is free.

For restaurant and attraction hours, recorded information is available on (407) 363-8000.

CityWalk has its own Guest Services outpost, which is well signposted and is by the restrooms. Also located nearby is **First Aid**.

Dining

CityWalk is filled with unique dining experiences allowing you to have a taste of Italy, New Orleans, Jamaica and the USA all in one place. Prices quoted for entrées are for adult meals; kids meals are much cheaper.

Quick Service:
Auntie Anne's Pretzel Rolls – Accepts Universal Dining Plan (snacks). Serves soft pretzels. A pretzel and a drink combo is $6 to $8.

Bread Box Handcrafted Sandwiches – Accepts Universal Dining Plan. Serves sandwiches and salads. Entrées are $6 to $12.

Burger King 'Whopper Bar' – No Universal Dining Plan. Serves burgers, wraps and sandwiches.

Cold Stone Creamery – Accepts Universal Dining Plan (snacks). Serves ice cream at $4.50 to $7.

Cinnabon – Accepts Universal Dining Plan. Serves cinnamon rolls and ice cream. Ice creams are $5 to $9.50.

Fusion Bistro Sushi & Sake Bar – No Universal Dining Plan. Serves sushi and sake, and drinks.

Hot Dog Hall of Fame – Accepts Universal Dining Plan. Serves hot dogs.

Entrées are $9 to $17.

Menchie's Frozen Yogurt – No Universal Dining Plan. Serves frozen yogurt priced at $0.59 per ounce (28g).

Moe's Southwest Grill – No Universal Dining Plan. Serves burritos, tacos, fajitas and other southwest dishes. Entrées are $4 to $8.50.

Panda Express – No Universal Dining Plan. Serves Chinese food.

Starbucks Coffee – Accepts Universal Dining Plan for selected snacks and beverages only. Serves coffees, ice-based drinks, sandwiches and pastries. Drinks are $2.70 to $5.

Table Service:

Antojitos Authentic Mexican Food – Accepts Universal Dining Plan. Serves Mexican-style food. Entrées are $13 to $31.

Bob Marley – A Tribute to Freedom – Accepts Universal Dining Plan. Serves Jamaican-style dishes. Entrées are $10 to $18.

Bubba Gump Shrimp Co – Does not accept Universal Dining Plan. Serves seafood and other dishes. Entrées are $12 to $29.

The Cowfish Sushi Burger bar – Accepts Universal Dining Plan. Serves burgers and sushi. Entrées are $10 to $28.

Emeril's Restaurant Orlando – Does not accept Universal Dining Plan. Serves Louisiana-style food. Entrées are $13 to $42. Menu differs at lunch and dinner.

Hard Rock Cafe Orlando – Does not accept Universal Dining Plan. Serves burgers, steaks, ribs and other American-style food. Entrées are $10 to $35. Serves breakfast.

Jimmy Buffet's Margaritaville – Accepts Universal Dining Plan. Serves Floridian and Caribbean inspired food. Entrées are $15 to $31.

NBC Sports Grill & Brew – Accepts Universal Dining Plan. Sports-bar style setting with 100 TV screens. Serves salads, and American-style food. Entrées are $11 to $40.

Red Oven Pizza Bakery – Accepts Universal Dining Plan. Serves pizza and salads from $11 to $14. Hands down the best pizza at Universal Orlando.

Pat O' Briens – Accepts Universal Dining Plan. A music venue that serves New Orleans-style dishes. Entrées are $9 to $18.

The Toothsome Chocolate Emporium – No Universal Dining Plan. A cool Steampunk chocolate factory with full Table Service meals and mouth-watering desserts. Includes take-out shake counter ($12.50 each).

Vivo Italian Kitchen – Accepts Universal Dining Plan. Serves Italian food. Entrées are $12 to $25.

Making Reservations:
To make reservations for Table Service restaurants, call (407) 224-3663 or visit opentable.com. Emeril's reservations are made directly on (407) 224-2424. Hard Rock Café Orlando priority seating can be requested online.

You can combine a meal at select locations with a Party Pass for $21 with tax and tip.

A meal plus mini-golf deal is also available for $25, and includes a meal from a select CityWalk location, and 18 holes of mini-golf at the *Hollywood Drive-In* course.

Top Tip 1: Most places have happy hours with discounted drinks and snacks. These vary between locations so ask staff for details.

Top Tip 2: Want free *CityWalk* valet parking? Most restaurants will validate your ticket for a two-hour stay between 11:00am and 2:00pm Monday to Friday. Emeril's will validate your ticket at any time. Tipping the valets is still customary.

Top Tip 3: Ask for the free Hard Rock Café VIBE tour and get an insight into the memorabilia and décor of the café. Available daily from 2:00pm to 9:00pm, simply ask.

Movie Theater

CityWalk features an *AMC Universal Cineplex* with 20 screens, including one that shows films in IMAX and IMAX 3D.

Ticket prices vary according to the time of day and several other factors.

A ticket for an adult is priced at $10.00 for shows before 3:55pm and $11.60 from then onwards. Children pay $8.40 all day. Showings on weekends and holidays before midday are $6.50.

Senior tickets for those aged 60 and over are $8.40 to $10.00. Annual pass holders get $3 off showings after 4:00pm.

There are additional charges for non-standard tickets. These are: $4 for a 3D movie, $5 for IMAX and $6 for IMAX-3D.

You can combine a standard movie ticket and a meal at select *CityWalk* restaurants for $21.95 including tax and gratuity.

Mini Golf

Hollywood Drive-In Golf is an adventure golf location with two different courses - one themed to sci-fi *(Invaders from Planet Putt)*, the other themed to horror movies *(The Haunting of Ghostly Greens)*.

The sounds, special effects, lighting and theming truly immerse you in the miniature world you are in. Pricing is $15 per adult and $13 per child. A single course takes between 35 and 45 minutes to complete, with each being made up of 18 holes.

The entrance is located next to the AMC Cineplex box office.
Discounts for Florida residents, military, seniors,

AAA members and Universal annual pass holders are available.

The mini-golf location is open from 9:00am to 2:00am daily.

Top Tip: Get your mini-golf tickets at least one day in advance at hollywooddriveingolf.com and save up to 13% per ticket.

Blue Man Group

The world famous *Blue Man Group* is the staple nighttime show at Universal.

The Blue Men create live music with makeshift instruments in a fun and hilarious musical adventure.

The show lasts 1 hour 45 minutes and does not have an interval. The show schedules change daily with no fixed start times. There are between 1 and 3 shows per day, with shows starting between 3:00pm and 9:00pm.

Ticket prices vary depending on the day of the week. Prices on this page do not include tax and are valid from Sunday to Thursday – add $10 per adult and $5 per child for Friday and Saturday shows. Higher prices apply daily during peak seasons.

A VIP experience is available for $200 per adult and $150 per child. It includes premier seats to the show, the experience includes a backstage tour loaded with

Blue Man Group history, a souvenir program and VIP lanyard, popcorn and soda, a merchandise discount, and an exclusive private meet-and-greet and photo opportunity with a Blue Man after the conclusion of the show.

Tickets can be purchased at the box office or by calling 407-BLUEMAN (407-258-3626) or online at blueman.com.

Pre-purchasing tickets can save you up to $10 per ticket. An Annual Passholder discount is available with

tickets starting at $60 for adults and $30 for children, plus tax.

Money-Saving Tips:
Students with a college ID or an ISIC card can get up to two "rush" day-of tickets for $34 each. AAA members can get a discount by showing their membership card.

Military members can also get a discount; visit your local MWR, ITT, and ITR offices to purchase. Buying in advance online will save you up to $10 per ticket.

	Tier 1	Tier 2	Poncho	Premium
Adult	$70	$85	$95	$105
Child	$30	$37.50	$42.50	$447.50

CityWalk Nightlife

As far as bars and nightclubs are concerned, you will find *Red Coconut Club, Pat O' Briens, CityWalk's Rising Star, the groove* and *Fat Tuesday*.

You will also find live music at *Hard Rock Live Orlando*. *Lone Palm Airport* is also an outdoor bar just across from *Jimmy Buffet's*.

If you fancy partying the night away, take advantage of the $11.99 *CityWalk* Party Pass (annual Passholders get 20% off up to 4 people).

The Party Pass allows you unlimited one-night access to all of the following locations: *CityWalk's Rising Star, Jimmy Buffett's Margaritaville, the groove, Pat O'Brien's, Red Coconut Club* and *Bob Marley – A Tribute to Freedom*.

Note: A party pass does not grant you entry during special ticketed events.

Without a Party Pass, the cover charge for a single nightclub is $7 - entertainment usually begins at 9:00pm. *Hard Rock Café* does not have a cover charge.

Top Tip: If you turn up before 9:00pm, you can avoid most cover charges.

For about $15, you can get the "*CityWalk* Party Pass + Movie ticket", which allows you entry to all the aforementioned locations plus entry into one movie

on the same day! This can be purchased at Guest Services.

Multi-day tickets and Flextickets include a free Party Pass that is valid for 14 days from first admission to the parks. So, multi-day ticket holders will not need to spend any extra to enjoy the nightlife.

Blue Man Show ticket holders can also use their ticket stub for free *CityWalk* club access.

CityWalk Shopping

If you fancy shopping, there are plenty of places to visit including: *Fossil, Fresh Produce, Quiet Flight Surf Shop, Element, The Island Clothing Store*, a

large *Universal Studios Store* (where you can get theme park gear without entering the parks) and *Katie's Candy Company*.

Finally, if you are in the mood for some ink, visit *Hart & Huntington Tattoo Company*.

For the Little Ones

It may be hard to imagine Universal Orlando as being a place for small kids when rides such as The Incredible Hulk Coaster and Dr. Doom's Fear Fall dominate the skyline. However, although Universal is by nowhere as kid-oriented as Disney's parks, there are still many activities dedicated to children.

Before leaving for the Universal Orlando Resort, we recommend you measure your child to avoid them getting excited about attractions they cannot ride.

There is nothing more disappointing than being slightly too short for a ride they have waited to do for months; ride operators will not bend the rules, even for half an inch, for everyone's safety. See the minimum height requirements for all attractions later in this section.

Remember that every child has a different comfort zone, and some may well be frightened of an attraction even if they do meet the minimum height requirements. Gently prompting and encouraging them to ride is fine; forcing them is not.

Important: Unlike at the Walt Disney World Resort, baby formula and diapers are not sold at the Universal parks.

Universal Studios Florida

The small members of the family will enjoy seeing Gru and the gang at *Despicable Me: Minion Mayhem* (40"/1.02m minimum) in a 3D simulator ride.

E.T. Adventure (34"/0.87m minimum) can be a little dark but is a relaxing ride – some kids may not enjoy the sensation of flying.

Woody Woodpecker's Nuthouse Coaster (36"/0.92m minimum) is a gentle roller coaster for starters.

The surrounding play areas in *Woody Woodpecker's KidZone* are great fun for kids, such as the *Curious George Goes to Town* play area.

For entertainment, kids are sure to love *A Day in the Park with Barney* - a live interactive stage show featuring the dinosaur himself, and the *Universal Superstar Parade* where they can see all their favorite characters.

The Simpsons Ride (40"/1.02m minimum) also features great characters. Note that this attraction may be frightening due to the large screen and simulated movements.

Islands of Adventure

Kids will love the *Seuss Landing* area with its play areas, meet and greets, and rides for all ages including the *Caro-Seuss-El; One Fish, Two Fish, Red Fish, Blue Fish* (under 48"/1.22m must ride with an adult); and *The High in the Sky Seuss Trolley Train Ride* (40"/1.02m to ride accompanied by an adult, or 48"/1.22m to ride alone).

In *Toon Lagoon,* you will find several water play areas to splash around in. *Me Ship, The Olive* is a fun play area here too.

Marvel Super Hero Island also features *Storm Force Accelatron* (an adult must accompany those under 48"/1.22m), this is a themed teacup ride.

The *Jurassic Park Centre* is also a fun, educational, place to learn about dinosaurs.

If the kids can't ride *The Hulk,* try *Pteranodon Flyers* (36"/0.92m minimum), *Flight of the Hippogriff* (36"/0.92m minimum) and *The Amazing Adventures of Spider-Man* (40"/1.02m minimum).

Ride Height Requirements

Many attractions at Universal Orlando have height requirements for guests' safety. We list all rides with height limits in ascending order, and what park they are in.

No Minimum Height:
• Shrek 4-D (USF) - No handheld infants
• Storm Force Accelatron (IOA) - An adult must accompany those under 48" (1.22m)
• One Fish, Two Fish, Red Fish, Blue Fish (IOA) – Children under 48" (1.22m) must ride with an adult

34" (0.87m)
• E.T. Adventure (USF)

36" (0.92m)
• Pteranodon Flyers (IOA) – Guests over 56" must be joined by someone under 36".
• Woody Woodpecker's Nuthouse Coaster (USF)
• Flight of the Hippogriff (IOA)
• The Cat in the Hat (IOA) – 36" to ride with an adult, or 48" alone
• Skull Island: Reign of Kong (IOA)

40" (1.02m)
• The Amazing Adventures of Spider-Man (IOA)
• Despicable Me: Minion Mayhem
•TRANSFORMERS: The Ride-3D (USF)
• The Simpsons Ride (USF)
• Race Through New York starring Jimmy Fallon (USF)
• The High in the Sky Seuss Trolley Train Ride (IOA) – 40" to ride with an adult, or 48" alone

42" (1.07m)
• MEN IN BLACK: Alien Attack (USF)
• Popeye & Bluto's Bilge-Rat Barges (IOA)
• Jurassic Park River Adventure (IOA)
• Harry Potter and the

Escape from Gringotts (USF)

44" (1.12m)
• Dudley Do-Right Ripsaw Falls (IOA)

48" (1.22m)
• Revenge of the Mummy (USF)
• Harry Potter and the Forbidden Journey (IOA)

51" (1.29m)
• Hollywood Rip Ride Rockit (USF) – Maximum of 79" (2.00m)

52" (1.32m)
• Doctor Doom's Fearfall (IOA)

54" (1.37m)
• The Incredible Hulk Coaster (IOA)

Understanding the Parks

Universal Orlando offers a variety of services designed to ease your day, from photo services to Express Passes, and Single Rider queue lines to package delivery.

My Universal Photos

My Universal Photos is a photo collection system that allows you to get all your in-park photos in one place.

You can get a *My Universal Photos* card from any in-park photographer. Each time you take a photo, simply hand the photographer your card - they will scan it and your photos will be grouped.

Before the end of the day, visit one of the *My Universal Photos* stores where you can choose the best pictures and have them printed.

You will need a new *My Universal Photos* card for each day of your vacation, unless you purchase a Photo Package. All in-park photos are deleted at the end of the operating day.

Although superficially the system seems to be fairly similar to Disney's Photopass system, there are not as many in-park photographers (though the number of on-ride photos is impressive).

Photo Package:
The *My Universal Photos* Photo Package is a way to pre-pay for all your in-park photos. When you buy the Photo Package, you will get two *My Universal Photos* cards on a lanyard that you scan any time you have your photo taken in the park.

All these photos are automatically uploaded to the *My Universal Photos* website where you can later download them.

My Universal Photos includes on-ride photos, character photos and in-park photographer photos on the same account!

To get a Photo Package visit the *My Universal Photos* stores at the entrance to each park – these are well signposted. Alternatively, after riding an attraction with an on-ride photo, visit the ride's photo desk to purchase the Photo Package.

You can use your Photo Package at the following locations:

Universal Studios Florida:
• On Location (Park Entrance Photos)
• E.T.'s Toy Closet & Photo Spot
• SpongeBob SquarePants Meet and Greet
• MEN IN BLACK Alien Attack
• Harry Potter and the Escape from Gringotts
• Shutterbutton's Photography Studio (with the Shutterbutton's package)
• Revenge of the Mummy
• Hollywood Rip Ride Rockit
• Donkey Photo Op (near Shrek 4-D)
• TRANSFORMERS Photo Op
• The Simpsons Photo Op
• Roaming characters where applicable
• Despicable Me Store Photo Op

Universal's Islands of Adventure:
• DeFotos Expedition Photography (Park Entrance Photos)
• Spider-Man Photo Op in Alterniverse Store
• In-Queue Photo Op at The Amazing Adventures of

Spider-Man
• The Incredible Hulk Coaster
• Dudley Do-Right's Ripsaw Falls
• Jurassic Park River Adventure
• Raptor Encounter
• T-Rex Automated Photo Capture in Jurassic Park
• Harry Potter and the Forbidden Journey
• The High In The Sky Seuss Trolley Train Ride! In-Queue Photo Op
• Roaming characters where available
• The Grinch Seasonal Photo Op

Photo Package Pricing:
There are a few different Photo Packages to choose from, depending on how long you visit (prices ex-tax):
• One day – $69.99 online, not sold in-park

• Three consecutive days – $89.99 online, and $99.99 in-park
• Fourteen consecutive days – $139.99 online, not available in-park
• Shutterbutton's Photo Package – $139.99 online

For most visitors, the 3-day package is the best value.

As well as the digital photos via a website, the price of the package also includes: the *Amazing Pictures* app to view your photos on your smartphone; and discounts on in-park ride photo prints.

The three-day package also includes these additional benefits: 1 free 5x7 or 8x10 print in a folder; 1 free 4x6 print; $5.00 5x7 or $10.00 8x10 prints at participating M*y Universal*

Photos locations; and $2.00 4x6 prints at participating locations.

The Shutterbutton's Photo Package includes unlimited Digital Downloads for 3 consecutive days; one 5x7 print; one 4x6 Print, and a Shutterbutton's DVD.

Annual pass holders pay $139.99 plus tax and get unlimited photos for the duration of their pass. In-park this will cost $10 more. This can pay for itself quickly.

Top Tip: To pre-purchase Photo Packages before you go, visit https://presale. amazingpictures.com/ UniversalFlorida.aspx. Certain options such as the 1-day and 14-day packages can only be bought online.

Package delivery

Universal Orlando's package delivery service allows you to purchase any item in the park and have it stored until later in the day when you can pick it up. This means you won't have to carry it around all day.

You can choose to have your purchase sent to on of two locations:

• **The front of the park** – By each of the theme parks' exit turnstiles you will see a small shop that is accessible both from inside and outside the park. Purchases made throughout the day are sent here for you to pick up. Allow 4 hours for delivery here.

• **Your hotel room** – You can also have the package

delivered straight to your hotel room if you are staying at one of the on-site hotels. It will be delivered the next day between 9:00am and 4:00pm. This service is unavailable the day before checkout or the day of checkout itself, so it is only suitable for stays of 3 nights or more.

The Universal Orlando app

The Official Universal Orlando Resort App, available for free on smartphones, allows you to: access wait times for all attractions when inside the parks, get directions to

attractions with step-by-step visual representations, see show times and special events, get custom wait time alerts, see park and resort maps, find guest amenities, see park hours,

set show time alerts, share on social media, and locate food items.

You can even buy park tickets and Express Passes right in this app.

Ride Lockers

Many of the rides at Universal do not allow you to take your belongings onto them; loose articles must be placed in free ride lockers.

How to use the in-park ride lockers:
• Approach a locker station. These are by the entrance to all rides that require their use;
• Select 'Rent a locker' from the touch screen;
• Put your fingerprint on the reader to be assigned a locker;
• Go to the locker, put your belongings inside and press the green button next to the locker to lock the door.

It is very important that you press the "lock" button to make sure the locker is actually locked! If you forget to press the green "lock" button, the locker will automatically lock 5 seconds after the door is closed.

The exception to this system is the new lockers for The Incredible Hulk where instead of using a fingerprint to verify your identity, you scan your park ticket instead.

The lockers are free for a certain period of time. This is always longer than the posted wait time. For example, a 90-minute queue for *The Hulk* would typically allow you 120 or 150 minutes of locker rental time to allow you to queue, experience the ride and collect your belongings.

If you keep your belongings in the lockers longer than the free period, charges apply. The charge is $3 for each additional 30 minutes, up to a maximum daily charge of $20.

Lockers for the water rides are not free - they are $4 for a set period (the wait time plus a margin), and $3 for each extra 30 minutes, up to a maximum of $20.

Top Tip 1: If your free locker time expires because the queue line took longer than expected, tell a Team Member. There should usually be a Team Member for each ride's lockers.

Top Tip 2: If you forget your locker number, a feature on the locker terminals can help you.

Top Tip 3: To avoid paying for a water ride locker, walk to another ride where lockers are free. *Forbidden Journey* often has long rental times, for example.

All-day park locker rentals:
Non-ride lockers are available at the entrance to each park – the cost is $10 per day for a standard locker or $12 for a family size locker. You may access these lockers as many times as you want throughout the day, though their non-central location can be a pain.

Universal's Express Pass

Universal Express Pass allows you to skip the majority of the queue lines in both parks for a fee.

The Express Pass is a card that allows you to enter a separate attraction queue line that is significantly shorter than the regular queue, and drastically reduces your wait times. For shows, you are allowed entry before guests who do not have an Express Pass – usually 15 minutes before show-time.

As a stand-alone product, Express Pass access costs between $40 and $150 per person per day. Use of the system is complimentary for those staying on-site at the *Hard Rock Hotel, Portofino Bay Hotel* and *Royal Pacific Resort*.

Which rides are not included?
Express Passes are valid on all attractions at both theme parks, with the following exceptions: *Ollivander's Wand Shop* (both IOA and USF) and *Pteranodon Flyers*.

How do I use it?
At an attraction entrance, show your Express Pass to the Team Member. They will scan it and you will be directed to a separate queue line from non-Express Pass guests.

Typical waits are 15 minutes or less for rides, even on the busiest days and are often shorter.

As you will be in a different queue line to the main one, Express Pass guests may

lose some of the storyline told in the queue. This is particularly evident on *Revenge of the Mummy*, *TRANSFORMERS, Escape from Gringotts* and *MEN IN BLACK*.

There are four types of Express Pass:
• *Universal Express Pass*: Available for purchase in the parks and online in advance. It allows one ride per participating attraction.
• *Universal Express Unlimited*: Available for purchase online and in the parks. It allows unlimited rides on each participating attraction.
• *Park-To-Park Ticket + Universal Express Unlimited*: Available for purchase online or over the phone (407-224-7840) and includes a regular park admission ticket for both parks and *Universal Express Unlimited* access every day. These tickets are available in one-day or multi-day versions. The ticket expires when all admission days on the ticket are used or 14 days after first use, whichever is first.

• *On-site Hotel Universal Express Unlimited Pass*: This is a perk for on-site hotel guests from the three most expensive hotels. It is included for each person in the hotel room for every day of their stay, including for all of the check in day and all of their check out day. It allows unlimited rides on each attraction. A photo of each guest will be printed onto this pass.

Each member of your party needs their own Express Pass. If you are not using an *On-site Hotel Universal Express Unlimited Pass* or a *Park-To-Park Ticket + Universal Express Unlimited*, you will need to purchase a separate Express Pass for each day of your trip.

How to Slash the Price of Express Passes:
As mentioned above, guests of select on-site hotels get *Unlimited Express Pass* access during their stay.

This means that staying at the *Hard Rock Hotel, Portofino Bay Hotel* or *Royal*

Pacific Resort is the best option if you want Express Passes for all of your stay. These are luxury resorts with fantastic amenities, located right next door to the theme parks. The queue-cutting privileges are a bonus!

Take a look at the money you can save: One night at *Royal Pacific Resort* during the busiest season (Holiday) for two adults is $424 including complimentary Hotel Unlimited Express Passes for your entire stay, including check-in and check-out days.

Buying the same Express Passes separately for these days costs $150 per person, per day. For two days, you would be spending $600 on Express Passes. So, by staying at the *Royal Pacific Resort* you will save just under $200.

The price gets even better when more people stay in the same room – one night for 4 people at the *Royal Pacific Resort* during the holiday season costs $454. In this case, your hotel stay would save you $800 on the cost of Express Passes. Even if you don't need the hotel room, it is cheaper to book one, check-in, get your Express Passes and leave straight away.

If you are a family of five, you can get roll-away beds at the on-site hotels for an additional $25 per night, reducing the price per person per day.

Savings are available year-round. During the Value Season in late January, two adults will pay $244 for a one-night stay at the *Royal Pacific Resort*. The Express Passes for these dates cost $70 per person, per day. You will save $36. Four adults would pay $294 for one night, saving $266 on Express Passes over two days.

Generally, stays longer than one-night become poorer value as these hotels do have expensive nightly rates. To take full advantage of this tip, you should only stay on-site for one night. Two days is usually enough to see everything on offer with Express Pass access! If you do want to stay longer, then we'd recommend spending the other days at a cheaper on-site hotel.

Do I need an Express Pass?
During peak periods, getting an Express Pass is almost essential. It guarantees you will not need to wait hours in queue lines. However, Express Passes are expensive and will often double the cost of your visit.

Having said this, with careful planning, time and by following our Touring Plans, you should be able to do most rides without an Express Pass, even during busy seasons.

If you are visiting outside of the peak periods of school breaks and holidays, then an Express Pass is not as beneficial. Outside of peak periods, you often do not need to wait more than 20 to 30 minutes for most attractions.

To do both parks in one day, you'll need Express Passes.

Finally, if you get an Express Pass, we recommend the 'Unlimited' version. You want to ride attractions as many times as you wish, not just once each.

If you can't afford it, skip the Express Passes. The money saved can feed you all day. You will not miss out by not getting an Express Pass if you get up early and follow our touring plans – you will wait, but you will save hundreds of dollars too.

Top Tip 1: Do not buy Express Passes in advance unless the parks will be busy. If unsure, wait until you are at the parks to see the wait times; this way you can make an informed decision.

Top Tip 2: If buying Express Park tickets at the parks, don't buy them from the kiosk outside the park gates – the queue here is usually longer than inside the park.

Top Tip 3: At certain times of the year, there are 'after 4:00pm' Express Passes sold for $40. Ask for these, as they are not advertised.

Top Tip 4: The *Park-To-Park Ticket + Universal Express Unlimited* ticket bundle is cheaper than buying park admission and the Unlimited Express Pass separately.

Top Tip 5: The free Hotel Express Pass only applies during regular park hours. During events where a separate admission ticket is required, such as *Halloween Horror Nights*, you will need to buy an event-specific Express Pass.

Child Swap

Sometimes when visiting a theme park, two adults want to ride an attraction but have a child that is not tall enough. Universal Orlando has a solution that allows you to take turns riding, but only queue once – Child Swap.

Simply ask a Team Member at an attraction entrance to use Child Swap.

Generally, one or more adults go in the standard queue line while another adult is directed to a child swap waiting area.

Once the first group has queued up and ridden the attraction, they proceed to the Child Swap area. Here the first group stay with the child, and the person who sat with the child gets to ride straight away, without having to wait in the queue.

This procedure may vary between attractions and can be combined with Express Pass – ask Team Members at attraction entrances about the specific procedure.

Stroller and Wheelchair Rentals

Both theme parks offer stroller, wheelchair and motorized ECV rentals.

The rental area is located to the left hand side of each park's turnstiles.

Rentals Prices (per day):
• Single Stroller – $15
• Single Kiddie Car – $18

• Double Stroller – $25
• Double Kiddie Car – $28
• Wheelchairs – $12, plus a $50 deposit.
• ECVs – $50 plus a $50 deposit.

The kiddie car is a stroller designed to look like a car with an enclosed front foot area, to stop kids slipping

out. It also has a steering wheel to play with.

ECVs must be operated by a single person aged 18 years old or over.

Wheelchairs can also be rented in the parking rotunda area.

Q-Bot Ride Reservation System

Q-Bot is a ride reservation system that is a more affordable alternative to Express Pass. The Q-Bot system is available anywhere that Express Pass can be purchased and is valid on all Express Pass rides, but it cannot be used for shows.

The system is managed on a portable device called a Q-Bot, which you rent for the day. It allows you to make ride reservations.

How does it work?
The Q-Bot is *not* an instant front of the line access system. Unlike Express Pass, this system does not get you onto rides faster; instead,

it allows you to virtually reserve a place in the queue line.

For example: The time is currently 14:00 and the wait for *Revenge of the Mummy* is 40 minutes.

You select *Revenge of the Mummy* on your Q-Bot and make a reservation – in this example, the reservation would be for 14:40 (the current time plus the wait time).

At 14:40, you can go to the

attraction and enter through the Express Pass queue line – this line will get you onto the ride quickly, but may take up to 15 minutes during peak periods.

While you are waiting for your reservation time, you can visit another attraction or show in the regular queue line, or shop, eat, etc.

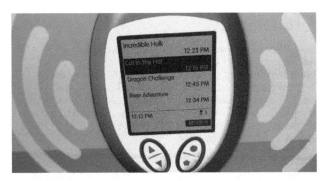

Used efficiently, you can double the number of rides you experience per day and spend a lot less time in queue lines.

Our favorite way to use the Q-bot is to make a reservation for a ride and then use that time to watch a show – this way you don't feel like you are waiting.

One great feature of the Q-Bot is that you can make ride reservations on the device wherever you are in the park, without needing to be physically present at a particular attraction to reserve. This means, for example, that you could be having lunch and make a reservation for *Despicable Me: Minion Mayhem*.

Do not cancel your reservation as you walk up to each attraction, the ride operator will validate your Q-Bot and then allow you access to the Express Pass queue.

For rides where you must stow your belongings in lockers, go to the ride entrance first, the attendant will validate your Q-Bot and you will be given a slip of paper to return to the Express Pass queue with, after you have stowed your belongings (including the Q-Bot).

Cancelling reservations:
You may cancel reservations at any time on the device, and you can have one active reservation at a time.

To make another reservation, you must ride the reserved attraction or cancel your reservation.

Back to our previous example: You can ride *Revenge of the Mummy* any time from 14:40. It is 14:40 now. You cannot reserve another ride until you ride *RoTM* or cancel the reservation.

If you cancel a reservation, it is the equivalent of you leaving the queue line – you lose your place, and if you later want to reserve for the same ride, you must wait the full wait time virtually.

What are my options?
There are two versions of Q-Bot – one allows one reservation per ride, the other allows unlimited reservations, so you can re-ride using Q-Bot.

Is it worth it?
Given the option of Express Passes or Q-Bot and an unlimited supply of money, of course the Express Passes win, as you get on rides in a maximum of 15 minutes – and usually in less than 5. However, if you have a more limited budget, and do not like waiting, then this may work well for you.

To make the most of the system, we recommend making Q-Bot reservations for the rides with the longest waits.

If you are visiting both parks in one day, and want to skip the waits at both, you will need to purchase one Q-Bot at each park which is a lot of hassle. In this case, we would recommend an Express Pass, despite the extra cost.

Note 1: Q-Bot is not offered daily. Often, only Express Passes are sold.

Note 2: When you purchase Q-Bot access, you will receive a voucher to be exchanged elsewhere. There, you sign a contract stating you will return the device, and provide credit or debit card payment details. You cannot use the Q-Bot system without a credit or debit card. If the Q-Bot is not returned or is damaged, you will be charged $50.

Single Rider

One of the best ways to significantly reduce your time waiting in queue lines is to use the Single Rider line instead of the regular queue line.

This is a completely separate queue that is used to fill free spaces on ride vehicles with guests riding on their own. For example, if a ride vehicle can seat 8 people and a group of 4 turns up, followed by a group of 3, then a Single Rider will fill the empty space on the ride vehicle.

This makes the wait times shorter for everyone in the park as all spaces on ride vehicles are filled.

Everyone benefits from the system: single riders typically get on much more quickly than the standard wait, and the regular queue line moves marginally quicker as all those single riders aren't in it!

If the parks do get extremely busy, then Single Rider lines can be closed. This happens when the wait in the Single Rider line is the same or greater than the regular line, thereby undermining its purpose.

If the Single Rider queue line is full and cannot accommodate more guests, it will also be temporarily closed.

If the park is almost empty, then sometimes Single Rider lines do not operate either, as there is no need for them.

Some rides have hidden Single Rider lines that are not advertised - in this case, simply ask the first attraction host you see (usually at attraction entrances) if the Single Rider queue line is open. If it is, then they will direct you accordingly.

One prime example of this is *The Harry Potter and the Forbidden Journey* Single Rider line, which can also be easily missed if you do not ask for it.

If you are travelling as a group, you can use the Single Rider queue line – just be aware that you will ride separately from the others in your party, but you can still meet each other after riding.

Single Rider lines are available on: *The Incredible Hulk, The Amazing Adventures of Spider-Man, Harry Potter and the Forbidden Journey, Jurassic Park River Adventure, Dr. Doom's Fearfall, Dudley Do-Right's Ripsaw Falls, Skull Island: Reign of Kong, Transformers: The Ride, Hollywood Rip Ride Rockit, Revenge of the Mummy, Harry Potter and the Escape from Gringotts,* and *Men in Black: Alien Attack.*

Guests with Disabilities

Visiting a theme park can be a complicated process for guests with disabilities but Universal Orlando has worked hard to give people in this situation as much of the full theme park experience as possible. Although, we cannot cover every kind of disability in this section, we have tried to include as much information as possible.

Universal Attraction Assistance Pass

A Universal Attraction Assistance Pass can really ease the day for some visitors. In order to obtain it, you will need to go to Guest Services (to the right through the turnstiles) and ask for the Attraction Assistance Pass.

Although it is not required, we strongly recommend a note from your doctor in English explaining exactly what help you need - whether it is avoiding waiting in the sun, standing for prolonged periods of time, or waiting in crowded areas. It all depends on your situation. Your doctor does NOT need to explain your disability, just what help you require in the theme parks.

The Universal Team Members at Guest Services will ask you several question to determine eligibility and what help you require. As mentioned, a doctor's letter is not required but will assist this process. You may then be issued an Attraction Assistance Pass and, if so, it will be explained to you.

Using the pass:
When you reach an attraction you would like to ride, show your Assistance Pass to the Team Member at the ride entrance.

If the wait time is less than 30 minutes, you will be immediately directed towards an alternative queue; this is often the Express Pass queue line.

If the attraction's wait time is at least 30 minutes, then the Team Member will write down a time on your Pass to return – we will call this a 'reservation' for the purpose of this guide.

When your reservation time comes around, show your pass at the ride entrance to be granted entry through the alternative queue. This is NOT a front-of-the-line ticket and waits can still be up to 15 minutes per ride.

You can only hold one ride 'reservation' at any time.

You may still enjoy accelerated entrance to attractions with less than a 30-minute wait, even with an active reservation.

If you want to change which attraction you have a reservation for, simply go to the next attraction and make a reservation with the attraction's greeter at the entrance. This will void your previous reservation.

An Assistance Pass allows up to 25 reservations; this is more than enough for a single day.

The Assistance Pass is valid for up to 6 people in the person's party.

Express Guest Assistance Pass:
The Express Guest Assistance Pass is used in situations when waiting in a queue or returning later is simply not possible, making the classic Universal Attractions Assistance Pass unsuitable.

As such, this pass is aimed at a much more limited number of guests and it is more difficult to obtain. This pass also does not require proof with a doctor's note, but a note may help. You may need to speak to a manager to obtain this card.

Generally speaking, the Express Guest Assistance Pass is for guests with certain mental health disorders, though a list of eligibility is not officially disclosed.

This Pass will allow you to enter the alternative queue instantly without needing to obtain a return time, no matter what the wait time is. This is NOT a front-of-the-line ticket and you must wait in the alternative queue.

The Express GAP is not valid at *Pteranodon Flyers* at *Islands of Adventure*. If you wish to visit this ride, then a classic Attraction Assistance Pass is necessary, or you will need to use the regular queue line instead.

Overall, this Pass acts very similarly to the Universal Express Pass Unlimited.

Other Assistance for Disabled Guests

Deaf/Hard of Hearing – For guests who are deaf or hard of hearing, many in-park shows have interpreted performances. The timing of these shows is printed on the regular park map.

Closed captioning and assistive listening devices, guidebooks for guests with disabilities, and attraction scripts are also available at Guest Services in each theme park.

Mobility Impairment and Wheelchairs – The whole of Universal Orlando has been designed to be as wheelchair-accessible as possible with ramps instead of steps. All shopping and dining facilities are accessible. Guests who would like to use a stroller as a wheelchair should ask for a special tag from Guest Services.

Outdoor stage shows also have designated areas for wheelchair users and their parties.

Most rides are accessible – some will require a transfer; others will allow you to ride in your wheelchair.

You can get a wheelchair at the parking rotunda to help with the considerable distance from the rotunda to the theme parks – simply ask the Team Members here. You can also rent a wheelchair inside the theme parks.

In using a parking rotunda wheelchair, guests may pay the additional cost for an ECV once at the parks or use this wheelchair throughout the day.

You do not NEED to have an Attraction Assistance Pass if you are in a wheelchair as all rides have an accessible entrance, but it can make things easier when there are particularly long queues, so we do recommend it.

If you, or someone you are with, suffers from a disability that is not visible, we thoroughly recommend the use of one of the Assistance Passes – without one you will need to use the regular queue line.

By its nature as a water park, accessibility at Volcano Bay is very limited for rides - you must be able to transfer for a wheelchair to the ride vehicle or slides and be able to climb many steps for most rides. ECVs are not permitted in queues or on rides.

Service Animals are permitted throughout the theme parks but each attraction will have a specific way of boarding. Kennels are available at some attractions for service animals.

The Team Members at the entrance of each attraction are able to provide more information.

Rides and shows: Special restrictions apply to guests with prosthetic limbs and guests with oxygen tanks.

More information about rides and shows specifically is available in the Riders Guide for Rider Safety & Guests with Disabilities (PDF file). It can be downloaded online at http://bit.ly/uordisab.

Dining

When visiting Universal Orlando, you will find an abundance of food options, from standard theme park fare to fine dining. However, eating somewhere you have never visited can lead to some uncertainty, especially for picky eaters, so this chapter aims to help.

Quick Service Universal Dining Plan

Guests wishing to plan their meal budget in advance may want to consider one of Universal's dining plans.

The Quick Service Universal Dining Plan is available to all guests and can be bought at any theme park Quick Service location, at UniversalOrlando.com or at dining reservation kiosks in the parks. It is accepted at over 100 locations throughout the Universal Orlando Resort.

Pricing
The cost of the Quick Service Dining Plan is $24.49 for adults and $15.98 per child. Prices include tax.

What is included?
Each day purchased on the Universal Quick Service Dining Plan entitles you to:
• 1 Quick Service meal – with Entrée and Non-alcoholic beverage.
• 1 Snack – From food carts or Quick Service locations such as popcorn, ice cream or a frozen beverage.
• 1 Non-Alcoholic Beverage – From food carts or Quick Service locations.

You will receive a voucher when you reserve your dining plan that can be exchanged for a dining plan card at the Ticket Centre or Guest Services at either theme park, or the Dining Reservation Cart at either theme park or *CityWalk*.

The Quick Service Dining Plan can be redeemed at all food locations owned and operated by Universal Orlando in *Universal Studios Florida, Islands of Adventure* and *Volcano Bay*, and at select *CityWalk* locations including *Hot Dog Hall of Fame* and *Bread Box* - a full list follows in this chapter.

Is it worth the price?
In our opinion, the Quick Service plan is not going to be a great purchase if you are looking for value for money. You have to try hard to profit from this dining plan by choosing the most expensive entrées on the menu every time.

Moreover, this isn't what we would classify as a real dining plan, as there is only one actual meal included – the rest are drinks and snacks. This will likely not be enough for most people.

If, however, you want to pre-pay your meals to help manage your budget, you may enjoy this option.

Top Tip: You can add a Coca-Cola Freestyle cup to this plan for $6 extra per day - this gives you unlimited soda refills for the day. More on these cups later in this chapter.

Universal Dining Plan

Unlike the Quick Service Universal Dining Plan, the Universal Dining Plan is only available to guests who have booked a vacation package through Universal Parks & Resorts Vacations or an authorized reseller – this includes both on-site and off-site hotels.

The Universal Dining Plan cannot be purchased at the theme parks.

The cost of the dining plan is $63.89 for adults and $24.48 for children (aged 3 to 9). Prices include tax.

Each day on the Dining Plan entitles you to:
• 1 Table Service meal – with Entrée, Dining Plan Dessert and Non-alcoholic beverage.
• 1 Quick Service meal – with Entrée and Non-alcoholic beverage.
• 1 Snack – From food carts or Quick Service locations. E.g. popcorn, ice cream or a frozen beverage.
• 1 Beverage – From food carts or Quick Service locations.

For those familiar with the Disney Dining Plan at Walt Disney World, this is very similar but there is one crucial difference: whereas at Disney you have to purchase a Dining Plan for the entire stay, (e.g. an 8-day stay would mean purchasing an 8-day Dining Plan), at Universal you buy however many days' worth of credits you need. So it would be possible to purchase 3 days' worth of food during an 8-day stay.

Credits are available for your entire stay. For example, with a 3-day dining package you would get 3 Table Service meal credits, 3 Quick Service meal credits, 3 Snack credits and 3 beverage credits.

With the Universal Dining Plan, you could split these throughout the duration of your stay. You could have a Table Service meal one day and a snack, and then have two Quick Service meals another day.

Character fans can also use one Table Service credit for the *Superstar Character Breakfast* at *Cafe La Bamba* - each worth $35.

The Universal Dining Plan can be redeemed at most food locations owned and operated by Universal Orlando in *Universal Studios Florida* and *Islands of Adventure* and *Volcano Bay*, and at select *CityWalk* locations - a full list follows. On-site hotel restaurants are not on the Dining Plan.

Guests who purchase the Dining Plan will receive a voucher when booking their vacation to be exchanged in the theme parks or *CityWalk*. The voucher can be exchanged for a card at the Ticket Centre Desk or Guest Services at either theme park, or Dining Reservation Carts at either theme park or *CityWalk*. It can also be collected at on-site hotels.

Is it worth it?
The Dining Plan is a good option for food lovers, but compared to Disney's system it still has a few niggles to work out. Firstly, exchanging a voucher for a card is time consuming.

Secondly, Dining Plan restaurants in *CityWalk* are limited – all the other restaurants are inside the theme parks, so you will need park admission each day. Frustratingly, as the on-site hotels are operated by Loews and not Universal, on-site hotel restaurants are not included in the plan.

Thirdly, each card has its own credits and operates independently. As such, a parent wanting to get four ice creams needs all four cards, and each ice cream is processed separately. Credits are not grouped like the Disney Dining Plan.

Having mentioned all these caveats, it *is* a good system. If you like having all your meals pre-paid with one less expense to worry about, and enjoy Table Service meals, then this is the perfect plan for you.

This plan generally offers better value than the Quick Service dining plan, especially if you eat the most expensive items on the menus, meaning that you can save money here.

Note: Gratuities are extra and not included in the price of the Dining Plan.

WHERE CAN I USE MY DINING PLAN?

Universal Studios Florida:
Snacks – *San Francisco Pastry Company, San Francisco Beer, Bone Chillin', Monsters Slush, Production Central Food, Auntie Annie's, Ben & Jerry's, Graveyard Popcorn, Louie's Fruit Stand, Starbucks, Florean Fortescue's Ice-Cream Parlour, The Fountain of Fair Fortune, King's Cross Station Kiosk, London Taxi Hut, The Hopping Pot, Expo Eat, KidZone Snacks, KidZone Pizza Company, Beverly Hills Boulangerie, Front Gate Popcorn, La Bamba Slush, La Bamba Veranda Bar, Schwab's Pharmacy* and *Silver Screen Coke*.
Quick Service – *Beverly Hills Boulangerie, Fast Food Boulevard, KidZone Pizza Company, Leaky Cauldron, London Taxi Hut, Louie's Italian Restaurant, Mel's Drive In, Richter's Burger Co.,* and *Universal Studios' Classic Monsters Café*.
Table Service – *Finnegan's Bar and Grill* and *Lombard's Seafood Grille*
Character Dining – *Superstar Character Breakfast at Café La Bamba*

Islands of Adventure:
Snacks – *Cinnabon, Croissant Moon Bakery, Port of Entry Fruit, Port of Entry Lemon Slush, Starbucks, Hop on Pop Ice Cream Shop, Moose Juice Goose Juice, Beer Cart, Oasis Coolers, Butterbeer Cart, Magic Neep Cart, all Jurassic Park Food Carts, Cathy's Ice Cream* and *ICEE*.
Quick Service – *Blondie's, Cafe 4, Captain America Diner, Circus McGurks Cafe Stoopendous, Comic Strip Café, Croissant Moon Bakery, Fire Eater's Grill, Green Eggs and Ham Café, Pizza Predattoria, The Burger Digs, Three Broomsticks, Thunder Falls Terrace* and *Wimpy's*.
Table Service – *Mythos Restaurant* and *Confisco Grille and Backwater Bar*
Character Dining – *The Grinch & Friends Character Breakfast (Seasonal)*

Volcano Bay:
Snacks – *Kora Poroka Ice Cream Kona, Lemon Slush, Dippin' Dots* and *ICEE*
Quick Service – *Kohola Reef Restaurant and Social Club, Whakawaiwai Eats, Bambu* and *The Feasting Frog*.
Table Service – No locations in this park.

CityWalk:
Snacks – *Auntie Anne's Pretzels, Cinnabon, Coke Icon, Cold Stone Creamery* and *Icon Hub Cart* and *Starbucks*.
Quick Service – *Bread Box Hand Crafted Sandwiches* and *Hot Dog Hall of Fame*.
Table Service – *Antojitos Authentic Mexican Food, Bob Marley: A Tribute to Freedom, Jimmy Buffet's Margaritaville, NBC Sports Grill, Pat O' Brien's, The Cowfish, Red Oven Pizza Bakery* and *Vivo Italian Kitchen*.

Refillable Drinks and Popcorn

Popcorn:

Refillable popcorn buckets are a great snack option if you are a big eater. You pay $5.99 for the popcorn bucket, and then can get as many refills as you want for $1.29 (plus tax) each.

There are four places at each theme park where your souvenir bucket can be refilled: just look for the big popcorn machines – these are usually outdoors. There are no popcorn refills at *CityWalk*, or at the on-site hotels.

Popcorn refills are only available for standard popcorn; flavored popcorn is not discounted and must be purchased at full price.

Coca Cola Freestyle:

Coca Cola Freestyle is a refillable drinks system. Here, you pay $14.99 plus tax for a Coca Cola Freestyle cup. You can then visit any of the 18 Coca Cola Freestyle locations - you will find them inside restaurants and as freestanding machines too - and refill your cup for free as many times as you want during that day. The cup has an RFID chip that, when activated, allows free refills.

There are over 100 different Coke drink mixes you can choose from at the machines, or you can stick to the standard Coke products.

You must wait 10 minutes between refills to discourage sharing. Additional days can be added for $5.99 per day.

Coke Freestyle stations at *CityWalk* and at Universal's on-site hotels are separate to this system.

Dining Reservations

When you want to sit down and have a Table Service meal in a busy theme park, you do not want to be kept waiting. Each minute you wait could be used to meet characters, watch shows or ride attractions. This is where dining reservations come in.

Unlike at Disney, at Universal you will not have trouble making dining reservations. Simply browse through the various restaurants and their menus on the Universal Orlando website, and book your table via OpenTable, whenever you want, at no cost to you.

With the exception of very busy seasons, you should be able to get a reservation for almost every restaurant a week or so in advance.

If there is a specific place you want to eat, we recommend you book your table as early as possible.

We have known to get same-day reservations, but don't count on it.

Top 5 Table Service Restaurants

Universal has Table Service restaurants dotted across its theme parks, *CityWalk* and the on-site hotels, and finding the best one can be tough. Luckily, we have rounded up those that you really should not miss out on below.

Note that prices and menus change all the time with seasons and chefs - those listed were correct as of when we last ate at the locations and should be taken as examples only.

1. Mythos (Islands of Adventure) – *Mythos* is often rated as the number one theme park restaurant in all of Orlando, let alone just Universal. This place is a pure delight to eat in, with its lavish interior, exotic menu and rather fair prices. This restaurant will truly transport you to a different world.

Entrées are $13 and $23. The food ranges from sandwiches to Shortribs, and Asian Salmon to Mahi Mahi. Note: *Mythos* is often only open for lunch.

2. Finnegan's Bar and Grill (Universal Studios Florida) – *Finnegan's* is always a fun place to dine, or to simply go inside for a quick drink. Themed as an Irish Pub, there is a lot of fun to be had, as well as some delightful treats.

Entrées are $11 and $22. The food includes sandwiches, Fish 'n' Chips, Beef Stew and Sirloin Steak.

3. Confisco Grille & Backwater Bar (Islands of Adventure) – Located in the *Port of Entry* area, *Confisco Grille* has a traditional range of theme park food, which may be better for families with younger children who are not quite ready to eat the Mahi Mahi at *Mythos*. It has a laid-back atmosphere.

Entrées are $9 to $22. You will find wood-oven pizzas, sandwiches, pasta, fajitas and more on the menu.

4. NBA City (CityWalk) – Many ignore this restaurant when walking past, perhaps discounting it as tacky because of its basketball theme. Do not be one of the people that makes that mistake; NBA City has some great food on offer and the portions are huge!

The desserts, in particular, amazing – try the Cinnamon Berries and the fried cheesecake for an unforgettable end to a meal.

Entrées are $10 to $34. There is a wide selection of food on offer from chicken quesadillas to pizzas, jambalaya, shrimp, salmon, pasta, and much more.

5. Emeril's (CityWalk) – *Emeril's* is the most premium of the Table Service restaurants listed here, with prices to match. With New Orleans-inspired dishes, you can enjoy seeing your food be prepared in the open kitchen. Alternatively, indulge and book yourself into the Chef's private tasting room with space for ten people.

Entrées are $12 to $18 at lunch, and $24 to $36 at dinner. Food ranges from shrimps and grits, to calamari, lasagne and the 18-oz ultimate rib-eye steak.

Top 5 Quick Service Restaurants

There are times that you may not want a three-course meal, preferring to use the time to watch a show, walk around the parks or ride your favorite attraction again.

Here are our favorite on-site Quick Service restaurants to make the most of your park time.

1. Three Broomsticks (Islands of Adventure)

– Everything about this restaurant puts it at the top spot: the atmosphere, the food and its opening hours. *Three Broomsticks* is open for breakfast, lunch and dinner, and is the only fully-fledged restaurant at *The Wizarding World of Harry Potter - Hogsmeade*.

Entrées are $9.50 to $17. Breakfast entrées come from around the world: England, the USA and Continental Europe just to name a few locations.

Lunch and dinner revolves around British dishes with some American classics too. You will find Cornish pasties, fish & chips, shepherd's pie, as well as smoked turkey legs, rotisserie smoked chicken and spareribs.

2. Thunder Falls Terrace (Islands of Adventure) –

This is another restaurant where the atmosphere adds to the experience. Step foot into *Thunder Falls* and you are in the middle of the world of Jurassic Park - and you get a spectacular view of the *River Adventure* ride splashdown from the restaurant's huge glass windows.

Entrées are $13 to $16. On sale are cheeseburgers, ribs, smoked turkey legs, wraps, and rotisserie chicken. The portion sizes are large for a theme park.

3. Louie's Italian Restaurant (Universal Studios Florida)

– As far as pizzas and pasta go inside the theme parks, *Louie's* does it best. It should be noted that there is not a huge variety of food on offer at Louie's and it is not particularly healthy.

Entrées are $7.50 to $14. You can also order a full pizza pie to share for $32 to $35.

Food includes spaghetti and meatballs, pizza and fettuccine alfredo. The meatballs and pizzas are the best we've had at a theme park Quick Service location.

4. Leaky Cauldron (Universal Studios Florida)

– This location has a great atmosphere inside, and like its other *Wizarding World* companion in this section, you can get some good British grub including Banger's and Mash, Cottage Pie, Toad in the Hole, Fish and Chips, etc. Entrées are $9.50 to $20.

5. Croissant Moon Bakery (Islands of Adventure) –

The food here is far from your standard theme park fare. This is a bakery and not somewhere to go for a full-blown lunch or dinner meal, but where you might go for breakfast or a snack.

Entrées are $2.50 to $12.50. Serves continental breakfasts, sandwiches, Paninis and great cakes! If you fancy a coffee, this is the place to visit too!

Tips, Savings and More

This section covers various ways to make your trip better - from ways to save time and money, to Early Park Admission and character meets.

Money Saving Tips

Take food in with you
Universal allows you to bring your own food into the parks. Whether it is a bag of chocolates or a drink, you can purchase these items at a fraction of the price anywhere outside of Universal property.

For drinks, why not put them in a cooling bag (hard-sided coolers are not allowed in the parks), and/or freeze them to drink throughout the day. Food should be fine in a backpack throughout the day.

Glass containers and bottles are not permitted in the parks.

Bring rain gear
There is a high likelihood that at some point during your Universal Orlando theme park adventure you will get wet, whether it is on one of the water rides, or in one of the famous Floridian thunderstorms.

Either way, we recommend you bring rain protection from home - either a raincoat, a poncho or even an umbrella (beware of lightning and umbrellas).

This saves you 1) from purchasing these items in the theme parks at inflated prices, and 2) wearing wet clothes when you get soaked.

Those big human dryers outside the water rides that you can pay $5 to go into are not very effective – don't waste your money.

Buy tickets in advance
Do not buy tickets at the gate – you will waste time and pay more than you need to.

As you are reading this guide, we can safely assume that you are planning to go, so there is no excuse not to buy your tickets in advance. You can do this over the phone, online at universalorlando.com or through a third party. You will save at least $20 per multi-day ticket by pre-purchasing them.

Plus, if you buy these tickets through the official Universal Orlando Resort website, you will receive a coupon booklet with up to $150 in money-off coupons.

In addition, some countries can get special deals, such as the UK where there is a 14-day ticket for at a discount on the official UK Universal Orlando website.

You do not NEED Express Pass
By following our Touring Plans, you will be able to see the majority of both Universal Parks in two days. If you have two full days, Express Pass simply is not a must: you can save up to $150 per person on Express Passes alone.

If you want to do everything in one day, Express Passes are necessary.

If you want Express Passes, stay on-site
The on-site hotels are more expensive than those off-site, but staying at select on-site hotels gets you unlimited Express Passes for

everyone in the room for the duration of your stay, including check in and check out days. To make the most of this, book a one-night stay at a Universal hotel.

On your check-in day, despite the fact your room may only be available from 3:00pm onwards, you can check in at any time, leave your bags and get your Express Passes. This means you can theoretically arrive at 7:00am or 8:00am, check in and head to the parks.

On your checkout day your Express Passes are valid until theme park closing, even after you check out. Express Passes are included in rooms at the *Hard Rock Hotel, Royal Pacific Resort* and *Portofino Bay Resort*.

Stay off-site
If you are on a budget, then stay off-site. There are many hotels just off Universal Orlando Resort property – a two to three-minute drive away, or a 15-minute walk.

These rooms can cost a fraction of the price of the on-site hotels. Plus, many do not have a nightly parking fee if you have a car.

Loyalty cards
AAA members, American Express Card holders and UK-based AA members all receive discounts throughout the resort. The AAA/AA discount is usually 10% at restaurants, though be sure to ask for it any time you pay.

Ride photos
Universal is pretty strict on you not taking photos of the monitors showing your on-ride photos.

As such, we recommend purchasing a Universal Photo Package – see the 'Park Services' chapter for more on this. It will pay for itself if you plan on buying just a few ride photos.

Stay at a partner hotel
Stay at one of Universal Orlando's partner hotels to receive in-room coupons. You may get Early Park Admission too.

Free lockers
Universal charges for lockers on water rides but not on any other rides. Simply, walk to a non-water ride and use those lockers.

If you will be doing this, be prepared to do a lot of walking to save a few dollars. Also be prepared to look around for the ride with the longest wait times to store your belongings at.

Both *Harry Potter and the Forbidden Journey* often has lockers with long access times.

Get *CityWalk* coupons
There is a completely free coupon book offering savings all across *CityWalk*.

You can get it from the small kiosk near the elevator between the two floors of *CityWalk*. You can also get dining information here.

Vouchers from here are generally for food, and offers vary throughout the year.

Operating Hours and Ride Closures

The Universal Orlando Resort is open 365 days a year and park operating hours vary according to demand.

On days when more visitors are expected, the parks are open longer; when there aren't so many visitors, the parks close earlier. The parks always operate for their advertised operating hours.

We strongly advise that you check opening hours in advance of your visit. Hours may change closer to the date of your visit, so do re-check again.

Park operating hours can be verified up to two months in advance at http://bit.ly/uorhours.

Ride refurbishments also happen throughout the year to keep rides operating safely and efficiently, and rides and attractions must close throughout the year to be renewed.

Refurbishments tend to avoid the busier times of the year.

Ride closures are only published a month or so in advance on the same page as the opening hours.

Remember that rides may close for technical issues or weather reasons. There is no reason to be angry at the ride attendants, as they do not control whether the ride runs or not.

How to Spend Less Time Waiting In Line

Park opening

Make sure you get to the theme park well before it officially opens. Ideally, you should be at the gate 30 minutes or more before opening. Remember it will take some time to park your car and get to the theme parks too.

Early morning is the least busy time, and in the first hour you can usually do 3 or 4 of the biggest rides - something that would take several hours during the rest of the day.

The parks often open earlier than advertised, particularly during busy periods.

Use Single Rider lines

If you do not mind riding separately from the rest of your party, use the Single Rider queue lines. See our section on these. They reduce your wait time significantly, so you can experience more each day; they are available at a surprisingly large number of major attractions.

Touring Plans

We have created expertly designed Touring Plans that tell you what order to do the attractions in; these have been crafted to let you see as much as possible.

Parades

Avoid attractions near the parade route immediately after the parade; they will be busier than usual.

The 59-minute rule

If Universal closes its parks at 9:00pm, that is when the queue lines (not the rides) close. Anyone in the queue line at park closing time is allowed to ride, no matter how long the wait is. If you have one final ride to do and it is getting to park closing time, get into the queue line before the park closes and you will still be able to ride.

This rule may not apply if an attraction has an exceptionally long wait time that would cause it to keep running for a long time after the park closing time.

Character Meet and Greets

Meeting characters can be one of the most enjoyable parts of the day in a theme park for many visitors. At Universal Orlando, there are many characters to meet and they usually have little-to-no queues.

At *Marvel Superhero Island*, you will usually find Captain America, Dr. Doom, The Green Goblin, Spider-Man, Storm and Wolverine. They even make their appearances (and disappearances) on cool quad bikes most of the time.

You can also meet the Seuss characters at *Seuss Landing* including Cat in the Hat, The Grinch, and Thing 1 and 2!

At *Universal Studios Florida* you will find the characters from The Simpsons including Bart, Lisa, Homer, Marge, Krusty the Clown and Sideshow Bob.

You will also find the Blues Brothers, the Men in Black, Shrek, Fiona and Donkey, Barney, SpongeBob, the Minions and Gru, and the Transformers characters regularly in areas outside their respective attractions.

Other characters also make appearances such as Scooby Doo and Shaggy, Lucy Ball, Woody Woodpecker, Betty Boop, and Marilyn Monroe.

Character schedules are in your park map. Some are not listed there but make appearances in the parks' Character Zones, located near the park entrance at *Universal Studios Florida*, and in *Toon Lagoon* at *Islands of Adventure*.

Early Park Admission

How about getting into the theme parks before other guests? Benefit from much shorter queue lines at select attractions, and an emptier park, with Universal's Early Park Admission (EPA).

During most of the year, Universal Orlando Resort offers one hour early entry to one of the two theme parks, plus Volcano Bay.

This benefit is available to on-site hotel guests and guests who have booked a Universal Vacation Package. It is available daily including check-in and check-out days.

At *Islands of Adventure* you will be able to access *The Wizarding World of Harry Potter: Hogsmeade* including all attractions (except *Hogwarts Express* which opens when *Universal Studios Florida* starts its operating day). *Caro-Seuss-el* in *Seuss Landing* is also usually available to ride.

At *Universal Studios Florida*, you can access *The Wizarding World of Harry Potter: Diagon Alley* and its attractions, minus the *Hogwarts Express*, which opens at the same time as *Universal's Islands of Adventure. Despicable Me: Minion Mayhem* is also available for Early Park Admission.

Early entry is offered daily for on-site hotel guests. Early Park Admission is also offered with vacation

packages booked through Universal whether staying on-site or not, as long as you have booked through Universal and purchased accommodation and park tickets together.

The park open for Early Park Admission is usually announced in advance on the Universal Orlando website. The web page may change or update as your trip approaches. During busier periods, both parks may be open early - during less busy periods, one of the two theme parks is open. In all cases, Volcano Bay is open for early admission in addition to the theme park(s).

How do I get Early Park Admission?
Guests staying at on-site Universal hotels show their room key to gain early admission to the parks.

If this is on your arrival date, then make sure you check in before Early Admission starts and go over to the parks; your room will not be ready but you will have Early Access to one or both parks.

You may be sent a text message with your room number later on. If you do not receive it, simply stop by the front desk to get your room number.

Guests with a Universal Vacation Package staying off-site do not need to check in to their hotel room. Simply go straight to the Will Call kiosks located by the entrance to each park.

Here you can enter your confirmation number given to you when booking to redeem your tickets with Early Park Admission.

We advise you bring your travel confirmation sent to you when you booked the package. This proves that you are entitled to this benefit in case there are any problems at the turnstiles.

Early entry is one hour before regular park opening – that is 8:00am most of the year (with the parks opening for regular guests at 9:00am), and 7:00am during peak seasons.

Universal Orlando vs Disney World

Universal is not the only theme park operator in Orlando. Far from it; if it were not for the Walt Disney World Resort, Universal Orlando most likely wouldn't even exist. There is no doubt that, one day, Universal would like to host just as many guests as Disney does. Here we compare both resorts.

Resort Size

Universal Orlando Resort is a needle in a haystack when compared to Walt Disney World. Disney covers 47 mi², an area twice the size of Manhattan. Universal Orlando in comparison is about 1 mi² in size. As a much smaller resort, there are both advantages and disadvantages.

Walt Disney World hosts four theme parks, two water parks, golf and mini-golf courses, almost thirty resort hotels, miles of roads, lakes, a shopping district and much more.

It is also important to note that Disney has only developed one third of its 47 square miles. Even so, Disney's currently developed real estate is about 15 times larger than Universal's.

Universal Orlando Resort has two theme parks, five resort hotels, and a shopping district, which is significantly smaller than Disney's.

This means that Walt Disney World Resort naturally has more things for guests to do; it has the scope to create larger developments – just *Disney's Animal Kingdom Park* alone is about 580 acres in size for example. All of Universal Orlando's land can fit in Animal Kingdom and its parking lot.

Due to the size restrictions, Universal has, been far more efficient than Disney with its space.

The sheer size of the resort also means that it can take a long time to get anywhere at the Walt Disney World Resort – you may be staying at an on-site hotel but it could be a 20-minute bus journey to a theme park.

Whereas, at Universal you are much closer to the action and can catch a boat to the theme parks from most hotels in a matter of minutes, or simply walk everywhere.

Lastly, because of its size you are much more likely to spend one, two or even three weeks at the Walt Disney World Resort, whereas you would struggle to fill more than four or five days at Universal Orlando.

Hotel Accommodation and Choice

The on-site hotels at Universal Orlando are physically much closer to the parks than those at Walt Disney World.

However, Universal has fewer choices and the three top hotels are expensive, though *Cabana Bay* and *Sapphire Falls* offer more moderate pricing.

The flip side is that Universal has off-site hotels located a 2-minute drive or a 15-minute walk away for a wider variety. At Walt Disney World off-site hotels are a good distance away.

You can actually walk off-site at Universal Orlando and leave the area. You can walk to a Walgreens

if you want; you can go and eat outside of the Universal Orlando Resort and make significant savings on the price of food; and vastly reduce the price of accommodation.

This is simply not possible at Walt Disney World without a car, and a lot more hassle.

Planning and The Off-Season

A visit to Walt Disney World involves *a lot* of planning. You will research the ticket type you need, the resort hotels you want to stay at (there are almost thirty to choose from), which theme park you want to visit on which day, and potentially have to book your restaurants 180 days before you even step foot on Disney property.

You then need a strategy about which rides to do when, know the ins and outs of the Fastpass+ system and know what times the characters meet and greet. You will even need to make ride reservations 30 to 60 days in advance to get the most out of your visit.

A Universal Orlando Resort vacation *does* require some planning. You know that because you have purchased this guide. It does, however, not require anywhere near the degree of planning that a Walt Disney World vacation does.

You can take it more at your own pace. There are only six on-site hotels to choose from, ticket options are simpler and restaurants can be booked much closer to your trip.

As far as having a strategy of what rides to do when, we recommend having one for all theme parks – Universal

Orlando included. However, you don't make ride reservations at Universal Orlando. Simply, follow our Touring Plans, or use Express Pass.

As well as planning, the off-season varies greatly between the two resorts.

At Walt Disney World, you can expect crowds year round. Some days are less busy days than others, but there is never a day at Walt Disney World when you can stroll onto *Seven Dwarfs Mine Train* in less than 5 minutes; it is never going to happen – especially at *Magic Kingdom*.

At Universal Orlando, there are still times of the year in the off-season when almost every ride is a walk-on – these are times when you can experience *Harry Potter and the Forbidden Journey* in a matter or minutes! The off-season still exists at Universal.

One of the reasons for this is that Walt Disney World appeals more to the local, retired population than Universal Orlando, so it attracts them year-round.

Having said this, if Universal Orlando continues to soar in popularity as it has done in recent years, it is very possible that the same situation will develop, particularly as the parks have a very limited number of attractions.

In 2016, for example, the Universal Orlando Resort theme parks welcomed 1 million more guests than they did the year prior. In 2015, there was an increase of over 2 million guests across the resort. The parks are getting busier at Universal, just not quite as busy as at Disney.

Innovative Attractions

This one will be controversial for Disney aficionados. In our opinion, Universal is developing more innovative and revolutionary experiences than Disney is nowadays.

Walt Disney World has some incredible experiences of its own - *Test Track, Soarin', Kilimanjaro Safaris, Rock 'n' Roller coaster, Flight of Passage* and *Tower of Terror* to name but a few.

However, the last big revolution for Disney, in our opinion, was *Expedition Everest* in 2006 – over ten years ago. If we wanted to be very generous, we'd include *Avatar: Flight of Passage* from 2017.

However, in the last decade, Universal Orlando has blown Disney out of the water. Universal only opened in 1990 and the resort is dotted with innovative experiences - *The Incredible Hulk Coaster* and *The Amazing Adventures of Spider-Man* win awards year after year. There is *Harry Potter and the Forbidden Journey, Harry Potter and the Escape from Gringotts, Hogwarts Express, Jurassic Park River Adventure, Skull Island: Reign of Kong* and more incredible experiences.

The attractions that have opened at Universal Orlando over the past few years are immense, and there are new attractions and experiences opening every year for the foreseeable future. Plus, if you are fan of water rides, whereas *Splash Mountain* at *Disney's Magic Kingdom* may get you a little bit wet, on Universal's water rides you will come out drenched. Universal *Universal's Islands of Adventure* is the perfect place get wet with three major water attractions.

Fastpass+ vs. Express Pass

At Walt Disney World, your park ticket enables you to make free Fastpass+ reservations to skip the regular queue lines by giving you a reserved ride time.

You can make reservations in advance or on the day of your visit and it is a good way of guaranteeing that you will experience some of your favorite attractions.

It is a slightly complicated system to understand but there are many resources

which explain the process.

Express Pass at Universal Orlando allows you near-instant entry to almost all attractions for a fee. This fee can be very high and up to $150 per person per day, but it is free if you are staying at certain on-site hotels.

Leaving aside that Disney's FastPass+ is much better value as it is free, Universal's Express Pass (because of its paid nature) works better:

there is rarely more than a 10-minute wait, you do not make reservations 30 to 60 days in advance, there is no complicated system to understand, fewer people use it and it is available for almost every single attraction.

It really is an 'express pass' at Universal Orlando because there's no need to make reservations, you simply turn up and skip the regular queue.

Employees

Although Universal Orlando has recently improved on the friendliness of Team Members, their employees are nothing like Disney's.

Disney's Cast Members are empowered to make "magical moments" to improve vacations in a way Universal employees cannot. Disney employees seem happier, and "courtesy" is one of 4 key values.

At Disney's parks, an employee's courtesy is only compromised in safety-critical situations. Otherwise, the Cast Members cannot do enough for you. Most will go above and beyond, and provide exceptional customer service.

Universal Orlando, on the other hand, provides good service and most of the Team Members are great but it seems that all too often these employees are overshadowed by those who are nonchalant at best, or rude at worst.

Experiences vary, but Disney has the edge.

Live Entertainment and Characters

For a company that is celebrating 100 years of movies, you would think that Universal would know how to put on a good show or two.

Shows like *SindBad* and *Fear Factor* are not relevant to the younger generation. In comparison, shows like *Finding Nemo: The Musical* and *Festival of the Lion King* are masterpieces.

It is the same story with parades and fireworks – although better than many other theme parks, Universal's offerings pale in comparison to Disney's parades or nighttime shows.

With characters, at Disney you need to plan character meets, even being able to make FastPass+ reservations. At Universal Orlando, its more spontaneous and you almost never have to wait more than 10 minutes to meet a character. Compare that to a 90-minute wait for the princesses at *Magic Kingdom* to see the difference.

Special Events and Nightlife

Universal and Disney keep people visiting all year-round with seasonal events. At Halloween, Universal offers scares with *Halloween Horror Nights*, Disney has a "not so scary" approach.

Christmas is a bigger deal at Disney World than at Universal Orlando. All four of the theme parks celebrate it with unique shows, decorations, lighting ceremonies and more. Even the hotels get into the spirit, with Christmas trees and gingerbread houses.

Universal Orlando holds its own unique events such as *Mardi Gras*. Disney celebrates the *Flower and Garden Festival*, and the *Food and Wine Festival*. Both celebrate the countdown to the New Year.

For nightlife, Universal hands down beats Disney.

Universal has a wider variety of clubs and bars, and is a real party scene. Walt Disney World does not do badly, with bars and a club at *Disney Springs*, but it is just nowhere near the scale of Universal Orlando's offerings.

Both resorts host a large-scale nighttime paid admission show – *Blue Man* at Universal, and *Cirque du Soleil* at Disney World.

Target Audience

One of the most striking differences between the two resorts is that Universal caters more towards teenagers and adults; Disney targets families.

With the exception of rides like *Rock 'n' Roller coaster, Tower of Terror, Expedition Everest, Mission: SPACE* and *Test Track*, there are few things that will get the adrenaline rushing for teenagers at Disney.

Disney caters towards families with experiences such as *Soarin', Big Thunder Mountain, Kilimanjaro Safaris* and character meets. Meanwhile, younger ones can enjoy rides such as *Peter Pan's Flight.*

Universal Orlando is very different. There are a few things for the younger members of the family, but

for the most part it is high intensity thrills that people come to Universal Orlando for, as well as big family adventures. *The Incredible Hulk Coaster, Hollywood Rip Ride Rockit* and *Dr. Doom's Fear Fall* are just a few of the thrill experiences on offer.

Family rides at Universal Orlando are generally more adult-oriented too: *Harry*

Potter and the Forbidden Journey and *Harry Potter and the Escape from Gringotts* are more thrilling than most rides at Disney.

There are attractions for smaller kids such as *Barney*, and playgrounds, but there are fewer of these at Universal.

Dining

Food at Universal Orlando is generally slightly cheaper than at Walt Disney World. However, there is not as much variety at Universal Orlando as at Walt Disney World; you will pretty much have to stick to standard theme park food.

The biggest difference in our opinion, however, is the quality and taste; while food at the Disney's parks is not gourmet by any standard, in general, it is much better than Universal Orlando's efforts.

There are also fewer Table Service establishments at Universal Orlando, so sit-down meal options are more limited.

At Disney, Character Buffets and Table Service meals are a big part of the experience.

Seasonal Events

Universal Orlando offers something different all year round. Whether it is live entertainment, horror mazes or Holiday cheer, the team have it all covered. This section covers all of the seasonal events that happen throughout the year.

A Celebration of Harry Potter

January 26th to 28th, 2018

The 'Celebration of Harry Potter' event is three full days of Wizarding fun.

Movie stars and autographs:
Several Harry Potter movie stars are present at the event each year.

Although the full list has not yet been announced, 2018 will include Stanislav Ianevski (Viktor Krum) and James and Oliver Phelps (Fred and George Weasley).

The events have been broadly similar over time, so the following information is from past events.

A Celebration of Harry Potter Expo:
Make your way through interactive displays in this unique collection of Harry Potter themed props, movie sets, artwork and more.

• *Harry Potter: The Exhibition* – Be sorted into your house in a Hogwarts-inspired setting.
• *Warner Bros. Studio Tour London: The Making of Harry Potter* – See the incredible behind-the-scenes talent that went into creating the iconic films.
• *MinaLima* – Graphic designers Miraphora Mina and Eduardo Lima display unforgettable artwork, including the Marauder's Map, Daily Prophet, and Hogwarts school books.
• *Pottermore and Audible* – Participate in an audio challenge that decides who knows the wizarding world inside-out. Plus, the latest news and announcements directly from J.K. Rowling's Wizarding World.
• *Scholastic* – A meet & greet and signing with Mary GrandPré, famed illustrator for the Harry Potter books.
• *Google Daydream VR Experience* – Google's virtual reality headset allows guests to experience the magic of *Fantastic Beasts and Where to Find Them* in VR. Wave a wand to solve puzzles and meet a few of the beasts in Newt's case.
• *Warner Bros. Interactive Entertainment* – Experience the Wizarding World in LEGO Dimensions and explore the worlds of Harry Potter, Fantastic Beasts and play as Hermione Granger.

Discussions & Demonstrations:
Guests can enjoy several panels and demonstrations:
• *Behind the Scenes: Harry Potter Film Talent Q&A* – Enjoy a fascinating and interactive Q&A session featuring your favorite Potter actors. Discover what it was like to work on one of the most successful film franchises ever.
• *Warner Bros. Studio Tour London: Creating Creatures* – Join special make-up effects artist Nick Dudman and discover how creature effects were brought to life in the Harry Potter series. •
Learn Wand Combat Skills with Paul Harris – This interactive panel offers you the chance to pick up your wand and take part in a live dueling masterclass. A Kids panel is also offered for guests ages 12 and under.
• *Stories from Harry Potter: The Exhibition* – A selection of some of the best known

authentic props used to create the entire film series. Eddie Newquist, creator of the exhibition, and Pierre Bohanna, head film prop-maker, tell stories of how these props and costumes were selected for exhibiting.
• *MinaLima* – MinaLima share insights into their role as graphic prop designers while working for 10 years on the Harry Potter movies, and more recently on *Fantastic Beasts and Where to Find Them*. They show some of the iconic props they created. They also discuss their involvement in The Wizarding World of Harry Potter - Diagon Alley.

Mardi Gras

February 3rd to April 7th, 2018

Celebrate New Orleans with Universal Orlando's Mardi Gras celebrations. Entry to Mardi Gras is included in your regular park admission.

The highlight of the festivities is the Mardi Gras Parade with colorful floats and incredible music. Enjoy the throwing of the beads from parade floats.

The Music Plaza stage hosts live acts on select nights. The line up for 2017 included: Ne-Yo, UB40, Olivia Newton John, Jason Derulo and many others. Concerts are all general standing room.

For the best view of the Music Plaza Stage concerts, you will need to skip the Mardi Gras Parade or watch it from near the Music Plaza stage area.

There are also New Orleans Bands in the French Quarter Courtyard, and stalls with local cuisine including jambalaya and gumbo. This area opens at 4:00pm and closes when the main concerts start.

After the parks are shut, head to the *CityWalk* bars and clubs for more New Orleans fun.

Top Tip: Note that when the parade starts, the regular shows and attractions at the park cease operating.

Rock the Universe

September 8th and 9th 2017. 2018 dates unannounced.

Billed as "Florida's Biggest Christian Music Festival", *Rock the Universe* is a whole weekend dedicated to Christian faith and worship, with Christian rock music.

As well as the main stage with Christian acts, the FanZone has more live music, as well as band autograph sessions, karaoke, and more. On Saturday night, guests can enjoy the Candle-lighting Ceremony.

There is also a free Sunday Morning Worship Service led by a guest speaker for those who hold *Rock the Universe* tickets.

Reservations are required.

Dates for 2018 have not yet been announced and the line-up is usually released in April each year.

Select attractions also operate during the event. In the past these attractions have included *TRANSFORMERS: The Ride-3D, Hollywood Rip Ride Rockit, Revenge of the Mummy*, and *MEN IN BLACK Alien Attack*.

Rock the Universe is a separate ticketed event that operates outside of regular park hours. 2017 tickets were priced at $65.99 for one night, or $103.99 for both nights. For $99.99 guests can enjoy both an all-day ticket on Saturday for either park, plus access to the concert in the evening.

Finally, for $164.99 guests can enjoy both nights of the event plus admission to the park for three full days with park-to-park access. These tickets offer fantastic value for money.

Top Tip: A one-night event-only Express Pass is available for $25 for one use per participating attraction, or $35 for unlimited uses at participating attractions.

Halloween Horror Nights

Select nights from September 15th to November 4th 2017

Halloween Horror Nights is an evening extravaganza with heavily themed scare mazes (a.k.a. haunted houses), live entertainment and scare zones where "scare-actors" roam around frightening guests. The theming is second to none and unlike any other scare attraction in the US. You will also find most of the regular attractions open inside *Universal Studios Florida*. *Halloween Horror Nights* has been running for over 25 years.

Universal warns the event "may be too intense for young children and is not recommended for children under the age of 13".

No costumes or masks are allowed at the event. This is nothing like Walt Disney World's "not so scary" Halloween parties. There is no trick-or-treating here; the idea is to scream.

Information on the 2018 event should be released in July and August 2018 but the general style of the event is similar each year.

Halloween Horror Nights (HHN) is very popular and *Universal Studios Florida* gets very crowded during this event.

On the busiest nights you can expect to wait 90 minutes or longer in line for each haunted house. Therefore, we highly recommend purchasing the HHN Express Pass if you want the full experience and to see everything, though it

is an additional supplement of over $100 per person. Even *with* the Express Passes waits can regularly reach an hour.

You will need to make several visits to see everything, especially without Express Passes.

Dates:
The 2017 event spanned 34 nights from September to November.

What is part of HHN?
Each year, the entertainment changes at Halloween Horror Nights, which keeps people coming back again.

For 2017, the following scare houses were available:
• American Horror Story
• Ash vs Evil Dead
• Dead Waters
• Saw: The Games of Jigsaw
• Scarecrow: The Reaping
• The Fallen
• The Hive
• The Horrors of Blumhouse
• The Shining

Guests can expect each house to last 3 to 5 minutes.

There are also scare zones, where characters roam the zones causing fear - here you do not need to queue to be scared - just walk through. In 2017, these were *Altars of Horror, Invasion!, The Festival of the Deadliest, The Purge* and *Trick 'r Treat*.

As far as live stage shows, 2017 saw *Bill & Ted's Excellent Halloween Adventure* (a really enjoyable stage show) and *Academy of Villains: Afterlife*.

The following attractions were also open during HHN in 2017: *TRANSFORMERS The Ride 3D, Hollywood Rip Ride Rockit, MEN IN BLACK Alien Attack, Revenge of the Mummy, The Simpsons Ride* and *Escape from Gringotts*.

Queues for rides are generally non-existent throughout the event, as the focus is on the scares. Guests with a HHN Express Pass can use it for both the scare mazes and the attractions.

Is The Wizarding World of Harry Potter part of HHN?

Halloween Horror Nights entertainment does not extend to the *Wizarding World of Harry Potter: Diagon Alley* area. This means that there will not be any 'horror' in Diagon Alley – no scare-actors, no shows, no haunted houses. The area is open in its normal state meaning that *Escape from Gringotts*, the shops and the eateries will be open. This is a safe refuge from the scares.

Pricing:

Ticket for 2018 are not being sold. For reference, in 2017 a single admission ticket to HHN was $78 or $86 depending on the date of your visit. There are many other ticket options.

HHN as an add on:

You can also one night of *Halloween Horror Nights* to your daytime park ticket and save money (versus purchasing each separately). Your *HHN* ticket does not have to be used on the same day as your daytime park ticket. The price in 2017 was $60 to $84 depending on the date of your visit. You can buy this in advance with a day ticket, or upgrade at the resort.

Rush of Fear Passes:

For online purchases made in advance, the *Rush of Fear* pass is great value at $91.99. It allows entry to every *HHN* night during the first 3 weeks for one price. A *Rush of Fear + HHN Express Pass* option was also available that allowed you entry during the first 3 weeks as well as allowing you to bypass the regular

lines once at each of the haunted houses every night – this was $300.

Other advanced purchase options in 2017 included the *Frequent Fear*, and *Frequent Fear + HHN Express Pass*, *Ultimate Frequent Fear (with/without) Express Pass* options. These were priced between $103 and $600, depending on the dates of visit and whether they include Express Pass access or not.

HHN Express passes:

If you wish to buy standalone HHN Express Passes, in 2016 these were $80 to $140 per person and valid during the event for haunted houses and attractions. We recommend you buy these in advance as they sell out.

On peak nights, you *need* a HHN Express Pass to see everything, as wait times for houses will typically be 90 minutes to 3 hours. Even with an Express Pass, you may have to wait an hour or more to enter the houses during peak nights – it is not instant entry.

Express Passes purchased for daytime at Universal Orlando are not valid during HHN, nor are the Hotel Express Passes.

RIP Tours:

You can get a VIP tour (an 'RIP' tour during HHN) with immediate unlimited access to every haunted house and park attraction (plus many other benefits) starting at $1599 for a party of 10. Tax and HHN admission are extra. A public RIP tour with one-time immediate access to each house, plus the attractions, is $160 per person; park admission is extra.

Daytime Guided Tours:

If you want to see how the horror of HHN is created without the scares, then Universal Orlando offers the *Unmasking the Horror Tour*, taking you on a lights-on walk through 3 haunted houses with a guide. You will learn about the creative process without the scares. Tours last 2 hours 30 minutes with up to 15 guests.

Tours are $80 per person - there are both morning and afternoon tours. Each tour goes through different houses – to see all six houses, it's $130 per person. Tours are held during regular park hours.

Call 1-866-346-9350 or email vipexperience@ universalorlando.com to book.

Grinchmas and the Holiday Season
November 18th, 2017 to January 1st, 2018

The Holiday season at Universal Orlando is filled with fun and the 2017 season is set to be bigger and better than ever before - with celebrations beginning a month earlier than last year and many new additions.

Information in this section is for 2017 - the event is broadly similar each year.

Thanksgiving
The theme parks do not hold special events for Thanksgiving, but the on-site hotels offer celebrations including buffets, and characters.

Christmas
At *Universal Studios Florida*, the *Universal's Holiday Parade featuring Macy's* rolls through the streets with floats from the world-famous Thanksgiving Day Parade in New York City. This event runs daily.

Mannheim Steamroller – the biggest selling Christmas band of all time – rocks the stage. In 2017, these take place on November 18, 19, 25, 26 and December 2, 3, 9, 10, 16 and 17.

At *Islands of Adventure*, you can watch *Grinchmas Who-liday Spectacular* – a 30-minute show with The Grinch, retelling the story of how he stole Christmas. You can meet Dr Seuss characters at the Holiday *Character Breakfast with Grinch and Friends* - reservations are required. You can actually meet The Grinch himself.

New for the 2017 Holiday Season is *Christmas in The Wizarding World of Harry Potter* - Hogsmeade and Diagon Alley are transformed by festive décor and special entertainment. And as the stars begin to shine, a stunning projection wraps Hogwarts castle in spectacular holiday spirit.

The fun continues at the on-site hotels with holiday dining, tree-lightings, live music, Hanukkah candle lightings, visits from Santa and Holiday movies.

There are no meets with Santa Claus at either park.

New Year's Eve
For the New Year, head over to *CityWalk* and party the night away with live performances and a midnight champagne toast! The New Year's Eve party is a ticketed event.

The New Year's Eve party includes admission to six clubs, six party zones, a pyrotechnics display, unlimited food, a midnight champagne toast and more. Tickets run at $110. Over 21s only. A VIP package is $185, plus tax.

Hard Rock Live Orlando hosts its own New Year Eve's party from 8:00pm, priced at $85 to $95 per person; $145 for VIP.

The theme parks are open late for New Year's Eve too.

The on-site hotels host their own parties with food, a DJ and more.

To make the most of your time at the parks, we highly recommend you follow one of our touring plans. These touring plans are not designed for you to have a leisurely, slow day through the parks; they are designed to get as much accomplished as possible, while still having a lot of fun.

How to use our Touring Plans

Due to the way our touring plans are designed, it may mean crossing the park back and forth to save you from being in long queue lines, but ultimately this extra walking means you can get the most out of your Universal Orlando Resort experience.

Generally speaking, our touring plans have you riding the most popular attractions (with the longest waits) at the start and end of the day when they are less busy; during the middle of the day, you will be visiting the attractions that have consistent wait times, and watching shows. This maximizes your time.

Touring with Express Pass:
These touring plans presume you do not have Express Pass access. If you do have this, then you are free to explore the park in whatever order you want, as you won't have to worry about waiting a long time for each attraction.

Touring without Express Pass:
At the moment, the Universal Orlando theme parks do not have an abundance of attractions

and wait times can be long throughout both parks. It is, however, perfectly possible to do all the rides in a single park on the same day with some planning.

We recommend you spend at least one day at each theme park, and then use a third or fourth day to re-do your favorite attractions at both parks, as well as any others you may have missed.

The key to making the most of these touring plans is to arrive at the park before it opens; that means being at the parking garages at least about 60 minutes before park opening if you are driving in. The parking garages open 90 minutes

before the first park opens.

If you want to buy tickets on the day, you will need to be at the park gates at least 45 minutes before opening. Otherwise, make sure to be at the park gates at least 30 minutes before opening with your park admission in hand. This is because the park regularly opens up to 30 minutes before the advertised opening time.

Using our Touring Plans:
Follow the steps in order. If there is a particular attraction you do not wish to experience, simply skip that step and then follow the next one - do not change the order of the steps.

1-Day Plan to Universal Studios Florida

Step 1: Be at the turnstiles with your park ticket in hand at least 30 minutes before the advertised park opening time. Proceed through the gates. Grab a park map and head towards *Despicable Me: Minion Mayhem*. Ride it. If the wait is longer than 30 minutes, we would skip this ride as the time you lose here really impacts the rest of your day.

Step 2: Experience *TRANSFORMERS: The Ride*. There is a Single Rider line. If you find that the wait is already very long, then we suggest you skip this step and ride *TRANSFORMERS* at the end of the day.

Step 3: Ride *Hollywood Rip Ride Rockit*. There is a Single Rider line available, though it moves slowly. At this time of the day, the regular stand by queue line should not be too long.

Step 4: Ride *Revenge of the Mummy*. A Single Rider line is available. We recommend the standard queue for the theming. Wait times rarely exceed 45 minutes.

Step 5: Experience *The Simpsons Ride*.

Step 6: Ride *Men in Black: Alien Attack*. A Single Rider line is available, which moves quickly.

Step 7: Have a Quick Service lunch to maximize your time.

Step 8: Watch *Universal's Superstar Parade*. You can get a good spot just minutes before it starts.

Step 9: Ride *E.T. Adventure*. Waits are usually less than 30 minutes.

Step 10: Watch *Universal's Horror Make Up Show*. This is our favorite live show. The theatre is fairly small so arrive about 20 minutes before the performance is due to start to be guaranteed a seat.

Step 11: Get in the virtual line for *Race Through New York Starring Jimmy Fallon*. When it is time to experience this, do so.

Step 12: See *Shrek 4D*.

Step 12.5: If Universal Orlando's newest attraction, *Fast and Furious: Supercharged* is open during your visit, experience this too by booking a place in the Virtual Line.

Step 13: Head to *The Wizarding World of Harry Potter: Diagon Alley*. You want to enter this area at least 3 hours before park closing. Crowds are lightest at the end of the day. Ride *Harry Potter and the Escape from Gringotts*, followed by a return journey on the *Hogwarts Express* (a Park-to-Park ticket is required to ride this). If you have the time, experience *Ollivander's Wand Shop*.

Step 14: Universal currently does not have a nighttime lagoon show but a new one is set to arrive in 2018, if this is being performed go and have a watch to end your day at the park.

Note: We do not include all park attractions here due to time constraints. Some attractions target young children such as *Barney* and *Woody Woodpecker* and may not be the most fun for your party.

If you have no interest in *The Wizarding World of Harry Potter*, it is possible to do almost every other attraction in the park in one day.

If you have Early Entry into *The Wizarding World of Harry Potter (WWOHP)*, you should explore this first, followed by this plan.

Step 1: Be at the park entry turnstiles with your ticket at least 30 minutes before opening. Go through the *Port of Entry* area.

Step 2: Turn left under *The Incredible Hulk Coaster*. Turn right and ride *The Amazing Adventures of Spider-Man*. Lines for *Spider-Man* build up quicker than *The Hulk's*.

Step 3: Ride *The Incredible Hulk Coaster*.

Step 4: Ride *Dr. Doom's Fearfall*.

Step 5: You should have done this within the first hour. Now, choose: either kids rides (Step 6 to 9) or water rides (Step 10).

Step 6: Ride *The Cat in the Hat* in *Seuss Landing*.

Step 7: Ride *One Fish, Two Fish, Red Fish, Blue Fish*.

Step 8: Head to *Seuss Landing* and ride the *High in the Sky Seuss Trolley Train Ride*.

Step 9: Ride the *Caro-seuss-el*. The wait is usually less than 10 minutes.

Step 10: Head to *Toon Lagoon* and do the three water rides. *Dudley's Do-Right's Ripsaw Falls* should be first, followed by *Popeye & Bluto's Bilge-Rat Barges*, and finally *Jurassic Park River Adventure*.

Step 11: Lunch. Save time with a Quick Service location. We advise eating outdoors, away from the A.C. after being wet.

Step 12: If you fit the limited ride requirements, ride *Pteranodon Flyers*. This will likely be one of the longest waits of the day.

Step 13: Experience *Poseidon's Fury* or *The Eighth Voyage of Sindbad Stunt Show*.

Step 14: Ride *Skull Island: Reign of Kong*.

Step 15: Now you only have a few minor rides left, as well as *Hogsmeade*. If there are at least 3 hours until park closing, follow the next steps. If there are less than 3 hours, you may want to head to *WWOHP* and step number 19.

Step 16: Watch *Oh, the Stories You'll Hear* in *Seuss Landing*.

Step 17: Explore *Camp Jurassic* near *Pteranodon Flyers*.

Step 18: Ride *Storm Force Accelatron*.

Step 19: Head to *WWOHP*. Ride *Flight of the Hippogriff*.

Step 20: Have dinner at *Three Broomsticks*.

Step 21: Experience *Ollivander's Wand Shop*. If you will be visiting *Universal Studios Florida*, skip this as they have a clone of this attraction at *Diagon Alley* with shorter waits.

Step 22: Ride *Harry Potter and the Forbidden Journey*. As long as you are in line before the park closes, Universal will let you experience the ride.

Top Tip: A common theme park trick is to post inflated wait times during the last operating hour to trick you into not queuing up for rides. Use your judgment. If the park is less busy now than it was in the middle of the day, then the waits will be much shorter.

Important: Queue lines usually shut at park closing time. However, if the wait times are extremely long (1 hour or longer), rides may shut early. Ask Team Members at an attraction towards the end of the day if they expect to close early.

In this touring plan, we show you how to hit the biggest attractions in both parks. It is not feasible to do all attractions at both parks in just one day, so we have only included the must-dos. This is a fast-paced plan.

You will need a Universal Orlando Park-to-Park ticket to access both parks on the same day.

Note: If you have Early Park Access, ride *Escape from Gringotts* first and then pick up the plan from Step 1. If you want to ride the *Hogwarts Express*, do so towards the end of the day.

Step 1: Be at the turnstiles of *Universal Studios Florida* with your ticket in hand at least 30 minutes before park opening, as queues build quickly. Proceed through the turnstiles, grab a park map, head straight ahead and ride *Despicable Me*.

Step 2: Experience *TRANSFORMERS: The Ride*. Use the Single Rider line to save time if you can.

Step 3: Ride *Hollywood Rip Ride Rockit*. Use the Single Rider queue line to save time if you can. You have now ridden three of the rides with the longest waits in this park.

Step 4: Ride *Revenge of the Mummy*.

Step 5: Lunch - we recommend *Monsters' Cafe* if you are staying in *Universal Studios Florida* and want a quick meal. A long Table Service meal will

undermine this entire plan.

Step 6: Make your way over to *Universal's Islands of Adventure*. Be prepared for long waits as this is the busiest point of the day. However, lines will still generally be shorter than at *Universal Studios Florida*, hence why we started there.

Step 7: Ride *The Incredible Hulk Coaster*. There is a Single Rider line available.

Step 8: If it is past 3:00pm, we recommend you skip this step. Otherwise, choose one of the following water attractions. Ride *Dudley Do-Right's Ripsaw Falls*, *Popeye & Bluto's Bilge-Rat Barges* or *Jurassic Park River Adventure*.

Step 9: Ride *The Amazing Adventures of Spider-Man*. Use the Single Rider line if possible to save time.

Step 11: Ride *Skull Island: Reign of Kong* if the wait is 45 minutes or less. In our opinion, it is not worth a longer wait.

Step 12: Explore *WWOHP: Hogsmeade*. Crowds will likely be lighter by now. Ride *Harry Potter and the Forbidden Journey*. The line should be substantially smaller than in the morning.

Step 13: Catch the *Hogwarts Express* over to *Diagon Alley*. If you are boarding the train 30 minutes or less before the park officially closes, you will have to move quickly to make it to the final ride.

Step 14: Proceed to *Escape from Gringotts*. As long as you are in the queue line before park closing, you will be able to ride, except in periods of extremely high crowds where the queue line may close earlier.

If time still remains, have dinner somewhere in the *Wizarding World* or elsewhere in the park.

Important: By leaving a major ride until the end of the day there is always the risk that you may not be able to ride if it breaks down.

The Future

The future of the Universal Orlando Resort looks bright with several projects currently in the works.

Fast and Furious: Supercharged – 2018

A new *Fast & Furious: Supercharged* attraction opens at *Universal Studios Florida* in 2018. This attraction will be located in the San Francisco park area.

Universal says: "This ride is going to fuse everything you love about the [Fast and Furious] films with an original storyline and incredible ride technology. You'll get to check out some of the high-speed, supercharged cars you've seen on the big screen."

"You'll be immersed in the underground racing world made famous in the films and explore the headquarters of Toretto and his team. Then, you'll board specially-designed vehicles for an adrenaline-pumping ride with your favorite stars."

We expect this new attraction to be similar to the Fast & Furious attraction in *Hollywood*, which consists of a tram filled with guests and a wraparound 3D screen with a chase

sequence as your tram moves in time with it. This ride will have a virtual like Jimmy Fallon's ride.

New "Aventura" On-Site Hotel – 2018

A new Value on-site hotel is coming in 2018.

The 16-story *Aventura* resort will be located right next door to *Loews Sapphire Falls Resort*, with a walking path and shuttle bus service to the theme parks.

As this will be a 'Prime Value'-priced hotel, there

will be no water taxi service to the theme parks or Express Pass access included with stays.

There will be a pool with a hot tub, bar and splash zone, a food hall with five different cuisines, a rooftop bar with stunning views, and much more.

And Much More

In 2016, Universal also bought large plots of land, which would be more than large enough to create a third and possibly even fourth theme park, as well as hotels. The land that *Wet 'n' Wild* stood on until December 2016 is also soon to be empty.

A live-action Terminator 3D show closed in 2017, as did a nighttime lagoon show and the Dragon Challenge roller coaster - we expect replacements for all of these attractions to arrive sometime in 2018 or 2019.

A Nintendo-themed land (Super Nintendo World) has also been announced to be coming, as well as one or two more hotels. There's even talk of a 5-acre expansion to Volcano Bay.

A Special Thanks

Thank you very much for reading *The Independent Guide to Universal Orlando 2018*. We hope this travel guide makes a big difference to your vacation and you have found some tips to save you time, money and hassle. Please leave us a review online.

If you have enjoyed this guide you will want to check out:
• The Independent Guide to Walt Disney World
• The Independent Guide to Universal Studios Hollywood
• The Independent Guide to Disneyland
• The Independent Guide to Disneyland Paris
• The Independent Guide to New York City
• The Independent Guide to Paris
• The Independent Guide to London
• The Independent Guide to Dubai
• The Independent Guide to Hong Kong
• The Independent Guide to Tokyo

Our theme park guide books give you detailed information on every ride, show and attraction and insider tips that will save you hours of waiting in queue lines! Our city guides are great overviews of fascinating locations with top attractions, good places to eat and stay, explanations of the transport system and much more.

Have fun at the Universal Orlando Resort!

Photo credits:
The following photos have been used in this guide under a Creative Commons attribution 2.0 license:
Universal Globe - Alison Sanfacon; Photos of all on-site hotels, Hollywood Rip Ride Rocket, Jimmy Fallon, Fast and Furious, Shrek 4-D, Cabana Bay Bus, Reign of Kong, Spider-Man ride and character photo, Nightlife/Rising Star, CityWalk Dining/Cowfish, Mini Golf, Universal Dining Plan, Antojitos, Quick Service photo, Tri-Wizard Tournament, Blue Man Group, Aventura Hotel, Cinematic Spectacular and Rock the Universe - Universal Orlando; Men in Black, Woody Woodpecker's Nuthouse Coaster, One Fish Two Fish, Storm Force Accelatron, Pteranodon Flyers and Single Rider - Jeremy Thompson; Animal Actors on Location, Planning/Staff and Express Pass, Character Meets with Sideshow Bob - Theme Park Tourist; Chad Sparks - Hogwarts Express; Diagon Alley - osseus; Q-Bot - accesso.com; Refillable Mug - Universal Orlando; Nintendo Logo - Nintendo Co., Ltd; Volcano Bay - Paulo Guereta; Diagon Alley - amyr_81; Height requirements - Theme Park Tourist

Cover Images: Hulk - Dave Walker, Springfield - 'osseous', Dinosaur and Grinchmas sign- Theme Park Tourist, IOA Panorama - John M, Macy's Holiday Parade - Jared; Volcano Bay - Paulo Guereta

HARRY POTTER, characters, names and related indicia are trademarks of and © Warner Bros. Entertainment Inc. Harry Potter Publishing Rights © JKR.

Universal Studios Florida Map

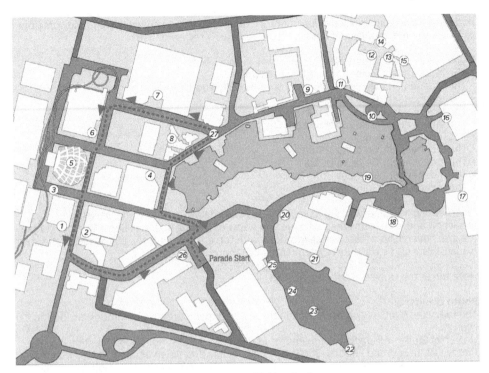

PRODUCTION CENTRAL
1. Despicable Me: Minion Mayhem
2. Shrek 4-D (Express)
3. Hollywood Rip Ride Rockit (Express)
4. 'TRANSFORMERS' The Ride: 3D (Express)
5. Music Plaza Stage
6. Jimmy Fallon: Race Through New York (Virtual Line)

NEW YORK
7. Revenge of the Mummy (Express)
8. The Blue Brothers Show

SAN FRANCISCO
9. Fast and Furious: Supercharged

THE WIZARDING WORLD OF HARRY POTTER - DIAGON ALLEY
10. The Knight Bus
11. Hogwart's Express - King's Cross Station (Express)
12. Knockturn Alley
13. Ollivanders
14. Harry Potter and the Escape from Gringotts (Express)

15. Live Performances

WORLD EXPO
16. Fear Factor Live (Express)
17. MEN IN BLACK: Alien Attack (Express)
18. The Simpsons Ride (Express)
19. Kang & Kodos' Twirl & Hurl (Express)

WOODY WOODPECKER'S KIDZONE
20. Animal Actor's On Location! (Express)
21. A Day in the Park with Barney (Express)
22. Curious George Goes To Town
23. Woody Woodpecker's Nuthouse Coaster (Express)
24. Fievel's Playland
25. E.T. Adventure (Express)

HOLLYWOOD
26. Universal Orlando's Horror Make-Up Show (Express)

ENTERTAINMENT
26. Universal's Superstar Parade

Islands of Adventure Map

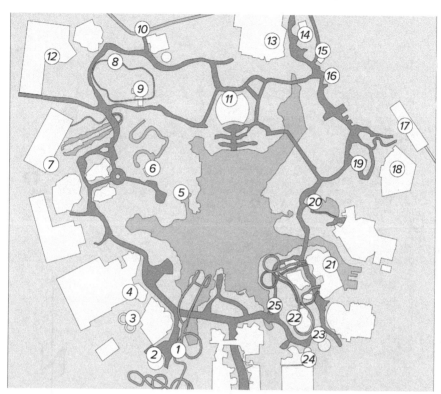

MARVEL SUPER HERO ISLAND
1. The Incredible Hulk Coaster (Express)
2. Storm Force Accelatron (Express)
3. Doctor Doom's Fear Fall (Express)
4. The Amazing Adventures of Spider-Man (Express)

TOON LAGOON
5. Me Ship, The Olive
6. Popeye & Bluto's Bilge-Rat Barges (Express)
7. Dudley Do-Right's Ripsaw Falls (Express)

JURASSIC PARK
8. Pteranodon Flyers
9. Camp Jurassic
10. Jurassic Park River Adventure (Express)
11. Jurassic Park Discovery Center

SKULL ISLAND
12. Skull Island: Reign of Kong (Express)

THE WIZARDING WORLD OF HARRY POTTER - HOGSMEADE
13. Harry Potter and the Forbidden Journey (Express)
14. Flight of the Hippogriff (Express)
15. Live Performances
16. Ollivanders
17. Hogwarts Express - Hogsmeade Station (Express)

THE LOST CONTINENT
18. The Eighth Voyage of Sindbad Stunt Show (Express)
19. The Mystic Fountain
20. Poseidon's Fury (Express)

SEUSS LANDING
21. The High in the Sky Seuss Trolley Train Ride! (Express)
22. Caro-Seuss-El (Express)
23. One Fish, Two Fish, Red Fish, Blue Fish (Express)
24. The Cat in The Hat (Express)
25. If I Ran the Zoo

Volcano Bay Map

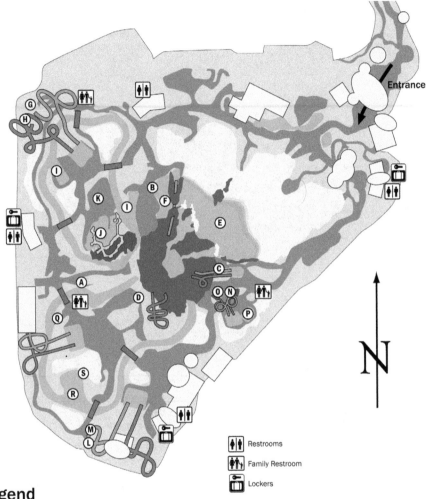

Entrance

N

Restrooms ♦♦
Family Restroom ♦♦
Lockers

Legend

KRAKATAU
A. Krakatau Aqua Coaster
B. Ko'okiri Body Plunge
C. Kala and Tai Nui Serpentine Body Slides
D. Punga Racers

WAVE VILLAGE
E. Waturi Beach
F. The Reef

RIVER VILLAGE
G. Honu
H. Ika Moana
I. Kopiko Wai Winding River

J. Runamukka Reef
K. Tot Tiki Reef

RAINFOREST VILLAGE
L. Maku
M. Puihi
N. Ohyah
O. Ohno
P. Puka Uli Lagoon
Q. Taniwha Tubes
R. TeAwa The Fearless River
S. Hammerhead Beach

CPSIA information can be obtained
at www.ICGtesting.com
Printed in the USA
LVHW06s1353090518
576440LV00033B/45/P